GROWING
STRONG IN
THE

SEASONS

GROWING STRONG IN
THE
SEASONS
OF LIFE:
AUTUMN

CHARLES R. SWINDOLL

FOREWORD BY
BILLY GRAHAM

WALKER AND COMPANY · NEW YORK

Large Print Edition by arrangement with Multnomah Press

First Large Print Edition published in the United States of America in 1989
    by Walker Publishing Company, Inc.

Published simultaneously in Canada by Thomas Allen & Son Canada, Limited, Markham, Ontario

Library of Congress Cataloging-in-Publication Data
Swindoll, Charles R.
    Growing strong in the seasons of life. Autumn / Charles R.
Swindoll ; foreword by Billy Graham.—1st large print ed.
        p. cm.
    Originally published in 1 vol.: Growing strong in the seasons of
life. Portland, Or. : Multnomah Press, c1983.
    Bibliography: p.
    ISBN 0-8027-2634-8 (lg. print)
    1. Devotional exercises. 2. Autumn—Religious aspects—
Christianity. 3. Large type books. I. Title. II. Title: Autumn.
[BV4832.2.S8852   1989]
242'.2—dc20   89-34703
                                                          CIP

Printed in the United States of America
10 8 6 4 2 1 3 5 7 9

With gratitude and delight I dedicate this volume to
EDGAR AND CANDEE NEUENSCHWANDER
who have been loving and supportive during the
cold winters, the changing springs, the hot
summers and the busy autumns of the
past twelve years of my life.
Through it all they have proven themselves faithful
friends both in season and out of season.

CONTENTS

Foreword   ix
Introduction   xi

AUTUMN
A SEASON OF REFLECTION

September
Doing vs. Being/4
The Final Priority/8
A Rabbit on the Swim Team/10
Self Praise/15
Monuments/19
Cracks in the Wall/23
Time/26
The Plug-in Drug/30
Please Be Careful/34
Resentment/38
Health/42
Isolation and Involvement/46

October
''The Opra Ain't Over''/50
Presumption/54
Designer-label Planet/58
Growing Old/62

CONTENTS

Reality/65
Lifelines/69
Adversity and Prosperity/73
Unambitious Leadership/78
Pharisaism/81
Fear/87
Courage/91
Songless Saints/95

November
Back to Basics/99
Busyness/103
Spiritual Leadership/107
A Fire for Cold Hearts/111
Biblical Illiteracy/114
Taking God Seriously/118
Nostalgia/122
Grace Revisited/125
Thanksgiving/129
Gentleness/134
One Long Extended Gift/138
Year-end Reflections/140

Conclusion   144
Footnotes   146

FOREWORD

On various occasions popular musical artists will release special albums that represent their best efforts. The titles are familiar to all of us: "The Best of Sinatra" . . . "The Best of Streisand" . . . "The Best of Neil Diamond." It is not uncommon for these albums to push their way quickly to the top of the hit parade as music lovers listen again and again to their favorite artists doing their best work.

This volume by your friend and mine could be called "The Best of Charles Swindoll." For almost ten years this man has ministered to our world through books, several of which have become (and still are) bestsellers. All of us have come to expect high quality and unusual insights as we pick up another book to which he has put his pen . . . and we have not once been disappointed.

Here is another winner. *Growing Strong in the Seasons of Life* is not only a beautiful statement about four distinct "seasons," it is also a healthy and balanced diet of hope for the discouraged, a refuge for the hurting, a challenge for the weary, and a friend for the lonely. You will smile with understanding and you may even weep with compassion. You will appreciate how carefully Scripture is woven into the fabric of each page, sometimes boldly, but more often softly, artistically.

May you find the living Lord opening His arms of love to you as you move through each of these four seasons. Take your time. Walk slowly. Feel God's presence as you consider the days and weeks and years that He has given to you. Ask Him to bring new strength to your soul.

With delight I recommend "The Best of Charles Swindoll" to you. Here is a combination of words, phrases, and ideas you'll want to read again and again. A book for all seasons.

Billy Graham

INTRODUCTION

I am glad God changes the times and the seasons, aren't you?

Just think how dull things would become if He didn't paint nature's scenes in different colors several times a year. With infinite creativity and remarkable regularity, He splashes white over brown and orange over green, giving such attention to detail that we are often stunned with amazement.

Each of the four seasons offers freshs and vital insights for those who take the time to look and to think. Hidden beneath the surface are colorful yet silent truths that touch most every area across the landscape of our lives. As each three-month segment of every year holds its own mysteries and plays its own melodies, offering sights and smells, feelings and fantasies altogether distinct, so it is in the seasons of life. The Master is neither mute nor careless as He alters our times and changes our seasons. How wrong to trudge blindly and routinely through a lifetime of changing seasons without discovering answers to the new mysteries and learning to sing the new melodies! Seasons are designed to deepen us, to instruct us in the wisdom and ways of our God. To help us grow strong . . . like a tree planted by the rivers of water.

This is a book about one of the seasons: spring. It offers a series of suggestions and ideas to help you read

God's signals with a sensitive heart. Quietly and deliberately, we'll walk together through each scene, pondering the subtle shading as well as the obvious broad brush strokes from the Artist's hand. Let's take our time and leave room for our feelings to emerge. Let's sing in harmony with the Composer's music. Let's drink in the beauty of His handiwork. It will take time, so let's not hurry.

Our hope is to grow stronger and taller as our roots dig deeper in the soft soil along the banks of the river of life. And let's not fear the winds of adversity! The gnarled old twisted trees, beaten and buffeted by wind and weather along the ocean shores, tell their own stories of consistent courage. May God make us strong as the winds whip against us, my friend. Rots grow deep when the winds are strong. Let's commit ourselves to growing strong in the seasons of life.

Just before we embark on our journey, allow me a final few paragraphs concerning the composition of these thoughts.

When my family and I moved to Fullerton in the summer of 1971, I immediately began writing a weekly column in our church newsletter, which I called "Think It Over." I have continued that discipline to this day. Little did I realize the far-reaching effect these provocative articles would some day have on our generation! I must express my gratitude to the staff of Multnomah Press for their creative sensitivity and bold vision to publish this material in various formats and titles since 1977. *For Those Who Hurt; Starting Over; Standing Out; Killing Giants, Pulling Thorns; Make Up Your*

Mind; and *Encourage Me* have emerged from the original "Think It Over" articles. We have all been amazed to see how broadly God has used and continues to use each one of those books in peoples' lives. I confess, *I have been the most surprised of all!* (I've been tempted to publish the letters from those who wrote me, describing how God used the books in their lives.) This volume is a compilation of several previously published articles that first appeared in those books, plus numerous other columns never before published. I am especially indebted to Julie Cave and Larry Libby for their loving friendship over the years. Because of their skilled insight and creative editorial assistance, I was able to see how such varied columns fit so beautifully into the theme of the seasons.

And once again, I declare my gratitude to Helen Peters, my personal secretary, for her unselfish patience with me, along with her relentless devotion to the task of typing and retyping the original manuscript.

Now . . . let's walk together as God escorts us through the seasons. Let's listen closely to His voice as we observe the changing scenery. It might be wise for us to brace ourselves against those strong gusts of wind that inevitably accompany each season. But even the storms bear a message of encouragement for us:

Deeper roots make for stronger lives.

Charles R. Swindoll

GROWING STRONG IN
THE
SEASONS
OF LIFE:

AUTUMN

O f all the seasons, autumn is my favorite. There's a feel about it, a distinct and undeniable aura that surrounds it. Being a football freak, I naturally would favor autumn. But of course it's much deeper than that.

Those leaves are part of it. What color, what artistry! Crisp, frosty mornings also help. What a refreshing change from oppressively hot afternoons and sweltering nights! Then there is a helpful return to routine as school starts. And along comes Thanksgiving, a nostalgic reminder that God has indeed "shed His grace on thee." The firewood is cut. The pumpkins are getting bigger. Our hearts are overflowing.

Let's think of autumn as a season of reflection. Time to gain new perspective. To stroll along the back roads of our minds. To think about what. And where. And why. Such visits through the museum of memory never fail to assist us in evaluating the way we were and establishing the way we want to be. This implies change, another reason autumn seems to represent a season of reflection. It's during this season the foliage changes. And the weather changes. And the time changes. Birds make their annual journey southward. Squirrels finish storing their nuts. Salmon start their phenomenal swim back to their spawning grounds. And many of the larger animals take their final stretch before curling up for a long winter's nap. With incredible consistency, all these creatures in the natural world act out their individual pageants without external instruction or some script to follow.

Quietly, without flare or fanfare, God graciously moves upon our lives, taking us from summer to autumn, a season when He mysteriously writes His agenda on the tablets of our hearts. Patiently He waits for change to begin. Without exception, it does. And we reflect on that as well.

Has autumn arrived in your life? Think before you answer. Close your eyes for a minute or so and consider what God has been doing deep within your heart.

Allow me to remind you of something you may have forgotten. It's a quotation from the New Testament:

> . . . God Who began the good work within you will keep right on helping you grow in His grace until His work within you is finally finished on that day when Jesus Christ returns (Philippians 1:6, TLB).

At the root of God's agenda is this promise. Think of it as a guarantee. The One who started "the good work within you" won't leave the task unfinished. At the end of the course, God won't get an "incomplete." For sure, He won't fail! Remember, it takes four seasons to make a year.

The autumn season of your life may be uncomfortable. Unemployment might be your lot. Or a broken romance. Perhaps you are grieving over a recent loss. Maybe you're lonely. Or hungry. Or cold. You feel anxious about those ugly clouds on the horizon that indicate an ominous tomorrow. The winds of adversity are picking up and you feel afraid.

Remember, "The roots grow deep when the winds are strong."

If autumn, the season of reflection, has come, expect your roots to deepen. Count on it. Yet, be assured of this, the Lord God *specializes* in roots. He plans to deepen you and strengthen you. But He won't overdo it. He is sovereignly and compassionately at work. We are more impressed with the fruit. Not God—He's watching over the roots. We like the product, He emphasizes the process. And painful though it may be, "He who began . . . will keep right on . . . until His work . . . is finished." So we can boldly declare, "Come wind, come weather, *welcome autumn!*"

If you have entered this season, may these "autumn thoughts" encourage and strengthen you.

Doing vs. Being

My high school graduating class had its thirtieth anniversary reunion a couple of summers ago. I'm sure they had a ball. A *blast* would better describe it, knowing that crowd. You gotta understand the east side of Houston back in the 1950s to have some idea of that explosive student body . . . a couple of thousand strong and a lot of 'em mean as a junkyard dog with a nail in his paw. Knife fights in the boys' washroom were almost as commonplace as fireworks in assembly, racial slurs in the hall, and beat-up Harley Davidsons in the alley.

Since I wasn't able to attend the reunion, I decided to blow the dust off my yearbook and stroll down nostalgia lane. Faces aroused smiles and stories as one memory after another washed over me. Funny, I remembered a project we seniors were given before the yearbook went to press back in '52. We were asked to think about the next twenty years and answer, "What do I want to do?" The plan was to record our dreams and goals in the yearbook, then evaluate them when we met again at each subsequent reunion . . . you know, sort of a decade-by-decade checkup. Some of the goals are not fitting to repeat, but some are both interesting and revealing.

4

Several said: "Make a million bucks."
Others:

- "Win all-American honors and play professional football."
- "Be the concertmaster of a symphony orchestra."
- "Own my own race car and win the Indy 500."
- "Rob Chase Manhattan Bank and escape to Fiji."
- "Finish medical school and have a practice in Honolulu."
- "Marry a rich movie star and live in Beverly Hills."
- "Become the world heavyweight boxing champion."
- "Sing at the Metropolitan Opera."
- "Make a living writing short stories, plays, and novels."
- "Travel abroad as a news correspondent."
- "Live fast, die young, and leave a good-looking corpse."

All sorts of goals. Some admirable, some questionable, some crazy, a few stupid.

Without wanting to sound needlessly critical, as I look back over three decades, I think we were asked to answer the wrong question. What we want to *do* is not nearly as important as what we want to *be*. And the longer I live the more significant that becomes. It's possible to do lots of things yet be *zilch* as a person.

Doing is usually connected with a vocation or career, *how we make a living*. Being is much deeper. It relates to character, who we are, and *how we make a life*. Doing is tied in closely with activity, accomplishments, and tangible things—like salary, prestige, involvements, roles, and trophies. Being, on the other hand, has more to do with intangibles, the kind of people we become down inside, much of which can't be measured by objective yardsticks and impressive awards. But of the two, *being* will ultimately outdistance *doing* every time. It may take half a lifetime to perfect . . . but hands down, it's far more valuable. And lasting. And inspiring.

Remember those familiar words from Colossians 3? Twice we read, "*Whatsoever you do . . . whatever you do . . .* " But then He immediately addresses things that have to do with *being*. Like being thankful, being considerate, being obedient, being sincere, being diligent. Same pattern—God emphasizes being more than doing.

So then, are you giving thought these days to things that count? I hope so. Goal-setting and achieving are important, especially if we are in need of being motivated. Moving in the right direction is a great way to break the mold of mediocrity. It's helpful to ask, "What do I want to *do?*"

But while you're at it, take a deeper look inside. Ask yourself the harder question, "What do I want to *be?*" Then listen to your heart . . . your inner spirit. True treasures will emerge. Pick one or two to start with. Don't tell anybody, just concentrate some time and attention on that particular target. Watch God work. It will amaze you how He arranges circumstances so that the very target you and He decided on will begin to take shape within you. Sometimes it will be painful; other times, sheer joy. It won't happen overnight, but that's a major difference between doing and being. One may take only twenty years; the other, the better part of your lifetime.

One can be recorded in a yearbook and is easily forgotten; but the other requires a lifebook, which is on display forever.

Deepening Your Roots
Ecclesiastes 2:11, 4:4; 1 Thessalonians 5:16

Branching Out
1. Look through your old high school yearbook. Think back to what you thought you'd be doing today.
2. Evaluate whether your lifestyle emphasizes ''doing'' more than ''being.'' If the answer is yes, seek to eliminate a ''doing'' to allow more time to develop the ''being'' part of you.

The Final Priority

Somebody copied the following paraphrase from a well-worn carbon in the billfold of a thirty-year veteran missionary. With her husband, she was on her way to another tour of duty at Khartoum, Sudan. No one seems to know who authored it, but whoever it was captured the essence of the greatest essay on love ever written.

If I have the language ever so perfectly and speak like a pundit, and have not the love that grips the heart, I am nothing. If I have decorations and diplomas and am proficient in up-to-date methods and have not the touch of understanding love, I am nothing.

If I am able to worst my opponents in argument so as to make fools of them, and have not the wooing note, I am nothing. If I have all faith and great ideals and magnificent plans and wonderful visions, and have not the love that sweats and bleeds and weeps and prays and pleads, I am nothing.

If I surrender all prospects, and leaving home and friends and comforts, give myself to the showy sacrifice of a missionary career, and turn sour and selfish amid the daily annoyances and personal slights of a missionary life, and though I give my body to be consumed in the heat and sweat and mildew of India, and have not the love that yields its rights, its coveted leisure, its pet plans, I am nothing, *nothing*. Virtue has ceased to go out of me.

If I can heal all manner of sickness and disease, but wound hearts and hurt feelings for want of love that is kind, I am nothing. If I write books and publish articles that set the world agape and fail to transcribe the word of the cross in the language of love, I am nothing. Worse, I may be competent, busy, fussy, punctilious, and well-equipped, but like the church at Laodicea—nauseating to Christ.

How about you and me committing ourselves to a life like this . . . a life that amounts to something . . . rather than nothing.

Each new day God brings our way is a fresh opportunity.

Deepening Your Roots
Matthew 12:33–37; John 17:20–26; 1 John 4:7–21

Branching Out
1. Love a missionary today by either writing him a letter, buying him a gift, sending a care package, calling long distance, etc.
2. Lift out a phrase from today's reading that convicted you and work at improving that attitude or action. Don't forget to seek God's assistance.

A Rabbit on the Swim Team

The Springfield, Oregon, Public Schools Newsletter published an article that caught my eye some time ago. As I read it, it struck me that I was reading a parable of familiar frustration in the Christian home and Body of Christ today.

Once upon a time, the animals decided they should do something meaningful to meet the problems of the new world. So they organized a school.

They adopted an activity curriculum of running, climbing, swimming and flying. To make it easier to administer the curriculum, all the animals took all the subjects.

The *duck* was excellent in swimming; in fact, better than his instructor. But he made only passing grades in flying, and was very poor in running. Since he was slow in running, he had to drop swimming and stay after school to practice running. This caused his web feet to be badly worn, so that he was only average in swimming. But average was quite acceptable, so nobody worried about that—except the duck.

The *rabbit* started at the top of his class in running, but developed a nervous twitch in his leg muscles because of so much make-up work in swimming.

The *squirrel* was excellent in climbing, but he encountered constant frustration in flying class because his teacher made him start from the ground up instead of from the treetop 'down. He developed ''charlie horses'' from overexertion, and so only got a C in climbing and a D in running.

The *eagle* was a problem child and was severely disciplined for being a non-conformist. In climbing classes he beat all the others to the top of the tree, but insisted on using his own way to get there . . .

The obvious moral of the story is a simple one—each creature has its own set of capabilities in which it will naturally excel—unless it is expected or forced to fill a mold that doesn't fit. When that happens, frustration, discouragement, and even guilt bring overall mediocrity or complete defeat. A duck is a duck—and *only* a duck. It is built to swim, not to run or fly and certainly not to climb. A squirrel is a squirrel—and *only* that. To move it out of its forte, climbing, and then expect it to swim or fly will drive a squirrel nuts. Eagles are beautiful creatures in the air but not in a foot race. The rabbit will win every time unless, of course, the eagle gets hungry.

What is true of creatures in the forest is true of Christians in the family; both the family of believers and the family under your roof. God has not made us all the same. He never intended to. It was He who planned and designed the differences, unique capabilities, and variations in the Body. So concerned was He that we realize this, He spelled it out several times in His final will and testament. Please take the time to read the thirty-one verses of 1 Corinthians 12 *slowly* and *aloud*.

Let's summarize some of these compelling truths:

God has placed you in His family and given you a certain mixture that makes you unique. No mixture is insignificant!

That mix pleases Him completely. Nobody else is exactly like you. That should bring you pleasure, too.

When you operate in the realm of capabilities, you will excel, the whole Body will benefit, and you will experience incredible satisfaction.

When others operate in their realm, balance, unity, and health automatically occur in the Body. But when you compare . . . or force . . . or entertain expectations that are beyond your or others' God-given capabilities, mediocrity or frustration or phoniness or total defeat is predictable.

If God made you a duck saint—you're a duck, friend. Swim like mad, but don't get bent out of shape because you wobble when you run or flap instead of fly. Furthermore, if you're an eagle saint, stop expecting squirrel saints to soar, or rabbit saints to build the same kind of nests you do.

I'll let you in on my own experience—the trap I fell into years ago. Having been exposed to a few of the "greats" in various churches and an outstanding seminary, I (like some of the other guys in the class) tried to be like *them*. You know, think like, sound like, look like. For over ten years in the ministry I—a rabbit—worked hard at swimming like a duck or flying like an eagle. I was a frustrated composite creature . . . like that weird beast in the second chapter of Daniel. And my feet of clay were slowly crumbling beneath me. It was awful! The worst part of all, what little bit of originality or creativity I had was being consumed in that false role I was forcing. One day my insightful and caring wife asked me, "Why not just be *you?* Why try to be like anybody else?" Well, friends and neighbors, this rabbit quit the swim team and gave up flying lessons and stopped trying to climb. Talk about relief! And best of all, I learned it was OK to be me . . . and let my family members be themselves. Originality and creativity flowed anew!

So relax. Enjoy your spiritual species. Cultivate your own capabilities. Your own style. Appreciate the members of your family or your fellowship for who they are, even though their outlook or style may be miles different from yours. Rabbits don't fly. Eagles don't swim. Ducks look funny trying to climb. Squirrels don't have feathers.

Stop comparing. Enjoy being you! There's plenty of room in the forest.

Deepening Your Roots

Song of Solomon 6:9; Isaiah 40:25–26; 46:5–9; 1 Corinthians 12:1–31

Branching Out

1. Identify one thing/action you are involved in that is forcing you to be something you're not. If possible, remove yourself from that activity and see if you sense relief.
2. When you compare yourself with others, what do you generally find you don't match up to? Now evaluate whether that's due to your trying to be something that simply is not you, or ever will be . . . and accept that.
3. Look at your friendships and determine if you're pressuring anyone to conform to your standards or skills. If so, back off, let the person be himself, and do something to encourage him to be himself.

Self-Praise

"Self-praise," says an ancient adage, "smells bad." In other words, *it stinks up the works*.

Regardless of how we prepare it, garnish it with little extras, slice and serve it up on our finest silver piece, the odor remains. No amount of seasoning can eliminate the offensive smell. Unlike a good wife, age only makes it worse. It is much like the poisoned rat in the wall—if it isn't removed the stench becomes increasingly unbearable. Leave it untouched and within a span of time it will taint and defile everything that comes near it.

I got nauseated last week. It wasn't from something I ate . . . but from *someone I met*. My out-of-town travels resulted in a short-term liberal arts education of self-praise to teach me some things I hope I never fully forget. This individual is a widely-traveled, well-educated, much-experienced Christian in his fifties. He is engaged in a ministry that touches many lives. He is fundamental in faith, biblical in belief, and evangelical in emphasis. For a number of years he has held a respected position that carries with it a good deal of responsibility and a great deal of time logged in the limelight. Such credentials deserve a measure of respect like the rank on the shoulders of a military officer or the rows of medals on his chest. Both merit a salute in spite of the man inside the uniform. In no way do I wish to diminish the significance of his position nor his record of achievement. But my point is this—he *knew* better . . . he had the ability to correct himself . . . but he chose to be, quite frankly, a pompous preacher!

You got the distinct impression that when the two of you were together, the more important one was not you. Little mistakes irked him. Slight omissions irritated him. The attitude of a servant was conspicuous by its absence. It was highly important to him that everyone knew who he was, where he'd been, how he'd done, and what he thought. While everyone else much preferred to be on a first-name basis (rather than "Reverend" or "Mister") he demanded, "Call *me* Doctor . . . " His voice had a professional tone. As humorous things occurred, he found no reason to smile . . . and as the group got closer and closer in spirit, he became increasingly more threatened. I confess that I was tempted to short-sheet him one night—or to order a Schlitz in his name and have it brought up to his room—or to ask the desk clerk to give him a call about 2:30 A.M. and yell, "Okay, buddy, out of the sack, rise and shine!" But I didn't. Now I almost wish I had. Just for the fun of watching the guy squirm!

Now let's get back to the basics. God says he *hates* "haughty eyes" (Proverbs 6:17). He calls a proud heart "sin" (Proverbs 21:4). He says if praise is going to be directed your way, "Let another praise you, and not your own mouth" (Proverbs 27:2). He drives home the message in Galatians 6:3:

16

. . . if anyone thinks he is something
when he is nothing, he deceives himself.

There is no greater deception than *self*-deception. It is a tragic trap laid for everyone, but especially vulnerable are those who have achieved . . . and start reading their own clippings the next morning.

Here's my advice. Three of the lessons I've earned since my encounter last week with Doctor Hot Shot are:

1. Get a good education—but *get over it*. Dig in and pay the price for solid, challenging years in school, and apply your education with all your ability, but *please* spare others from the tiring reminders of how honored they should feel in your presence.

2. Reach the maximum of your potential—but *don't talk about it*. Keep uppermost in your mind the plain truth about yourself . . . you have to put your pants on one leg at a time just like everybody else.

3. Walk devotedly with God—but *don't try to look like it*. If you are genuinely God's man or woman, others will know it.

Deepening Your Roots
Proverbs 21:4; Luke 18:9; John 12:42–43; Galatians 6:12–14

Branching Out
1. I dare you to remove all those diplomas from the wall in your office—or any object that promotes you and your achievements.
2. Check your ''pride quotient'' by listening and counting how many times you talk about yourself today. Whenever you hear the word ''I'' it's a clue you're patting yourself on the back.
3. Don't tell anyone about what *you* did this week that would indicate you've got a handle on your spiritual life. In other words, take on point three above.

Monuments

Not far from Lincoln, Kansas, stands a strange group of gravestones. A guy named Davis, a farmer and self-made man, had them erected. He began as a lowly hired hand and by sheer determination and frugality he managed to amass a considerable fortune in his lifetime. In the process, however, the farmer did not make many friends. Nor was he close to his wife's family, since they thought she had married beneath her dignity. Embittered, he vowed never to leave his in-laws a thin dime.

When his wife died, Davis erected an elaborate statue in her memory. He hired a sculptor to design a monument which showed both her and him at opposite ends of a love seat. He was so pleased with the result that he commissioned another statue—this time of himself, kneeling at her grave, placing a wreath on it. That impressed him so greatly that he planned a third monument, this time of his wife kneeling at *his* future gravesite, depositing a wreath. He had the sculptor add a pair of wings on her back, since she was no longer alive, giving her the appearance of an angel. One idea led to another until he'd spent no less than a quarter million dollars on the monuments to himself and his wife!

Whenever someone from the town would suggest he might be interested in a community project (a hospital, a park and swimming pool for the children, a municipal building, etc.), the old miser would frown, set his jaw, and shout back, ''What's this town ever done for me? I don't owe this town nothin'!''

After using up all his resources on stone statues and selfish pursuits, John David died at 92, a grim-faced resident of the poorhouse. But the monuments . . . it's strange. . . . Each one is slowly sinking into the Kansas soil, fast becoming victims of time, vandalism, and neglect. Monuments of spite. Sad reminders of a self-centered, unsympathetic life. There is a certain poetic justice in the fact that within a few years, they will all be gone.

Oh, by the way, very few people attended Mr. Davis's funeral. It is reported that only one person seemed genuinely moved by any sense of personal loss. He was Horace England . . . the tombstone salesman.[1]

Before we're too severe with the late Mr. Davis, let's take an honest look at the monuments being erected today—some of which are no less revealing, if not quite so obvious. A close investigation will reveal at least four:

- FORTUNE
- FAME
- POWER
- PLEASURE

Much the same as the Davis gravestone, these monuments are built in clusters, making them appear formidable . . . and acceptable. As the idols in ancient Athens, our society is saturated with them.

FORTUNE. How neatly it fits our times! Its inscription at the base is bold: "Get rich." The statuesque figures in the monument are impressive: a hard-working young executive; a clever, diligent businessman unwilling to admit to the greed behind his long hours and relentless drive.

FAME. Another monument tailor-made for Century Twenty. It reads: "Be famous." All its figures are bowing in worship to the popularity cult, eagerly anticipating the day when their desire to be known, seen, quoted, applauded, and exalted will be satisfied. Young and old surround the scene.

POWER. Etched in the flesh of this human edifice are the words: "Take control." These figures are capitalizing on every opportunity to seize the reins of authority and race to the top . . . regardless. "Look out for number one!"

PLEASURE. The fourth monument is perhaps the most familiar of all. Its message, echoed countless times in the media, is straightforward: "Indulge yourself." If it looks good, enjoy it! If it tastes good, drink it! If it feels good, do it! Like the line out of the Academy Award winning song "You Light Up My Life" that says:

> It can't be wrong
> If it feels so right . . .

Conspicuous by its absence is the forgotten philosophy of Jesus Christ. He's the One who taught the truth about being eternally rich through giving rather than getting. About serving others rather than leaving footprints on their backs in the race for the farthest star. About limiting your liberty out of love and saying no when the flesh pleads for yes. You know—the whole package wrapped up in one simple statement . . .

> . . . seek first His kingdom, and His righteousness; and all these things shall be added to you (Matthew 6:33).

No elaborate set of statues. No sculptures done in marble—not even an epitaph for the world to read. And when He died, few cared because few understood. They were too busy building their own monuments.

We still are.

Deppening Your Roots
Proverbs 11:7; Proverbs 11:16; Proverbs 28:28; Ecclesiastes 5:10–20; 1 Corinthians 4:18–21

Branching Out
1. Do something that shows you're not seeking control at home or on the job.
2. What keeps you from ''seeking first the kingdom of God''?

Cracks in the Wall

The longer I live the less I know *for sure*.

That sounds like 50% heresy . . . but it's 100% honesty. In my younger years I had a lot more answers than I do now. Things were absolutely black and white, right or wrong, yes or no, in or out, but a lot of that is beginning to change. The more I travel and read and wrestle and think, the less simplistic things seem.

I now find myself uncomfortable with sweeping generalities . . . with neat little categories and well-defined classifications. Take people, for example. They cannot be squeezed into pigeon holes. People and situations are far more complex than most of us are willing to admit.

- Not all Episcopalians are liberal.
- Not all athletes are thickheaded.
- Not all Republicans are Christian good guys.
- Not all collegians are rebels.
- Not all artists are kooks.
- Not all movies are questionable.
- Not all questions are answerable.
- Not all verses are clear.
- Not all problems are easily solved.
- Not all deaths are explainable.

Maybe the list comes as a jolt. Great! Jolts are fine

if they make you think. We evangelicals are good at building rigid walls out of dogmatic stones . . . cemented together by the mortar of tradition. We erect these walls in systematic circles—then place within each our over-simplified, ultra-inflexible "position." Within each fortress we build human machines that are programmed not to think but to say the "right" things and respond the "right" way at any given moment. Our self-concept remains undisturbed and secure since no challenging force is ever allowed over the walls. Occasionally, however, a strange thing happens—a little restlessness spring up *within* the walls. A few ideas are challenged. Questions are entertained. Alternative options are then released. Talk about threat! Suddenly our superprotected, cliché-ridden answers don't cut it. Our over-simplified package offers no solution. The stones start to shift as the mortar cracks.

Two common reactions are available to us. *One*: We can maintain the status quo "position" and patch the wall by resisting change with rigidity. *Two*: We can openly admit "*I do not know*," as the wall crumbles. Then we can do some new thinking by facing the facts as they actually are. The first approach is the most popular. We are masters at rationalizing around our inflexible behavior. We imply that change always represents a departure from the truth of Scripture.

Now some changes *do* pull us away from Scripture. They must definitely be avoided. But let's be absolutely certain that we are standing on scriptural rock, not traditional sand. We have a changeless message—Jesus Christ—but He must be proclaimed in a changing, challenging era. Such calls for a breakdown of stone walls and a breakthrough of fresh, keen thinking based on scriptural insights. No longer can we offer tired, trite statements that are as stiff and tasteless as last year's gum beneath the pew. The thinking person deserves an intelligent, sensible answer. He is weary of oversimplified bromides mouthed by insensitive robots within the walls.

Perhaps by now my words sound closer to 90% heresy. All I ask is that you examine *your* life. Socrates once said,

> The unexamined life is not worth living.

If you've stopped thinking and started going through unexamined motions, you've really stopped living and started existing.

That kind of "life" isn't much fun, nor very rewarding. I'd call it about 100% heresy . . . and only 50% honesty.

Deepening Your Roots
Matthew 15:9; Mark 7:1–13; Colossians 2:8–23

Branching Out
1. If you're the type who has a comment or opinion on everything, sometime today respond to a person by replying: "I don't know."
2. What's something you're resistant to? Is it a black and white issue that Scripture gives a clear-cut answer on, or is it an issue based solely upon tradition?

Time

We set our clocks back one hour last Saturday night.

Every time I mess around with that spring-up, fall-back routine, I smile. It always reminds me of the back-woods lady in Louisiana who wrote the government one summer complaining about this new fangled plan called daylight savings time. She argued, "That extra hour of sunshine done burnt up all my tomater plants."

It is rather remarkable how much difference one hour makes, even when you don't raise tomaters. It hits me abruptly when I look out my window in the late afternoon, expecting to see a mellow golden glow at dusk, but finding, instead, everything black. The opposite occurs at dawn. It will take all of us severald days to become accustomed to the switch. Funny, we'd never notice it if it were a gradual thing, like only a couple minutes a week. But it's sudden. Out of the blue we're a full hour into brighter mornings and darker evenings now that fall has fallen.

Time continues to be one of those intriguing subjects to me. On some occasions it seems so elusive, so slippery. Whoosh, there goes a week . . . *a month!* Yet there are other segments of time that pass with the speed of a glacier. And have you noticed how stubborn and

26

uncooperative time is? When you want time to zip on by, it drags. Then, when you want it to slow down to a crawl, it's tomorrow already.

Another thing: Time may be a great healer, but it's a rotten beautician. It's also terribly relative. Two weeks on a vacation, for example, is never the same as two weeks on a diet, is it? Also . . . some folks can stay longer in an hour than others can in a week. And have you noticed how quickly deadlines arrive, even though you try to push them away? On the contrary, isn't it amazing how slowly habits are broken, even though you desire to conquer them immediately?

And in every one of those situations, each hour had exactly sixty minutes—no more, no less.

I've just about come full circle with this time business. God alone is its Master . . . not us. He is the only One who "changes the times and the seasons" (Daniel 2:21). I especially like the way David put it:

> But as for me, I trust in Thee, O LORD, I say, "Thou art my God." My times are in Thy hand . . . (Psalm 31:14–15a).

Makes good sense. Since He has an "appointed time for everything . . . for every event under heaven—" (Ecclesiastes 3:1), an ideal method of time management is T-R-U-S-T, putting the pressure it brings back into His hand. That certainly beats the alternative! If you really mean it when you say, "Thou art my God . . . " then hand over to Him the things He alone can master. We could call it Operation Entrust.

● Is time dragging?　　　　　　　　　　TRUST

- Are deadlines arriving?   TRUST
- Those habits lingering?   TRUST
- That diet getting old?   TRUST
- Unwanted guests staying?   TRUST
- Beginning to look (and feel) older?   TRUST
- Prayers aren't being answered?   TRUST
- Recovery taking longer?   TRUST
- Employment lacking challenge?   TRUST
- Finances fading fast?   TRUST
- Promotion more remote?   TRUST
- Romance not blossoming?   TRUST
- Decisions getting complicated?   TRUST
- Dreams becoming distant?   TRUST
- School less satisfying?   TRUST
- Feeling unappreciated? Used?   TRUST
- Dreading winter?   TRUST

Maybe it will help to read again the psalmist's lines:

I say, "Thou art my God." My times are in Thy hand.

Want a practical suggestion? Cement those twelve words into the creases of your memory. Then, each morning for the rest of this month, right after you plant your feet beside your bed, look out the window and repeat those words out loud. Quietly, yet with feeling. If you want to get downright fanatical about it, you can even add on a prayer like:

Today, Lord, each hour is yours . . . not mine.
Whatever happens, I trust You completely.

But don't get too carried away with this predawn project. Enough is enough. Too much early morning devotion could make you miss breakfast and late for work. Several days like that back-to-back and you wouldn't have to sweat the time. In fact, you'd have all the time you needed without the hassle of employment!

Come to think of it, you could even get into raising tomaters . . . uh, if that extra hour of sun don't burn 'em up.

Deepening Your Roots
Psalm 40:1–4; Psalm 130:5–6; Proverbs 20:22; Daniel 2:19–23; Hebrews 6:13–15

Branching Out
1. What's something you feel pressured about? Are you trusting God with it? How about talking to Him right now about the pressure you're feeling.
2. Memorize, "I say, 'Thou art my God.' My times are in They hands." (Psalm 31:14–15a) and quote it each morning.
3. Name an area of your life that's hard to entrust to God. Trust Him with it today, tomorrow, and however long it takes for you to sense His—not your—control of it.

The Plug-in Drug

A fascinating experiment on addiction was reported in a recent issue of *Good Housekeeping* magazine.[2] Not drug addiction. Not alcohol addiction. Not tobacco or candy addiction. It was on television addiction.

A Detroit newspaper made an offer to 120 families in the city. The families were promised $500 each if they would agree not to watch TV for one month. That's right—500 bucks if they'd keep the tube turned off for just thirty days. Guess how many turned down the offer.

Ninety-three.

Of the twenty-seven families that said yes, five were studied and reported on in the magazine article. Right away you realize it was quite an adjustment for them. Each family had been watching television from 40 to 70 hours a week . . . that's between 5.7 and 10 hours *a day*. Think of it! Every day of every week the monotonous sounds and electronic pictures were a continual part of those household—year in and year out.

Serious pains accompanied the sudden, cold-turkey withdrawal from the plug-in drug. Remarkable things occurred, some almost bizarre. Like the lady who started talking to the cat or the couple who *stopped* talking to each other altogether!

But some good things also occurred. Books were pulled off the shelf, dusty from neglect, and read. Families played games, listened to the radio, and enjoyed playing records together. In one family two young kids spent some time practicing how to spell their names and addresses!

Miracle of miracles, several actually reported the younger kids took their baths at night without throwing a fit. And *some* (better sit down) willingly practiced their piano lessons.

The results? Well, the "no TV month" families finally had to admit four facts:

1. Their family members were brought closer together.
2. More eyeball-to-eyeball time between parents and children took place.
3. There was a marked increase in patience between family members.
4. Creativity was enhanced.

I would love to report otherwise . . . but I must be honest rather than wishful and add that television eventually won out once again. All five families returned to their addiction for nearly the same numbers of hours as before. Some *more*.

It's not the TV that disturbs me. No, it's just another gadget that can be used and enjoyed on occasion. It's the abuse that bothers me—the paralyzing addiction that stifles human creativity and cripples personal relationships. I agree with the comment made in the *Christian Medical Society Journal* a couple of years ago:

> The primary danger of the television screen lies not so much in the behavior it produces as the behavior it prevents.[3]

Turning on the television set can turn off the process that transforms children into people . . . and paralyzed viewers into thinking, caring persons. That's why the nine-year-old in San Francisco was overhead saying:

> "I'd lot rather watch TV than play outside 'cause it's boring outside. They always have the same rides, like swings and things.[4]

One reputable authority declares that children raised on television come to adulthood with no evident signs of decline in overall intelligence. There is apparently no huge brain drain, but there are a few peculiarities that concern the pros in this field.

- Increased communication in a near nonverbal speech ("like man . . . uh . . . you know . . . uh . . . ").
- Much less spontaneity and fewer imaginative concepts coming from young adults.
- An intense, almost irrational, dependence on music with a heavy beat as their only art form.
- The ever-present drug scene.
- Greater interest in passive experiences than those requiring mental interaction and active involvement.

Since television sets sit in ninety-seven percent of American homes (more homes have TV than indoor plumbing), these problems aren't decreasing.

Hey, let's do something about this, folks! It's a tough,

uphill battle, but it *isn't* insurmountable. Coming off the addiction is always hard. It actually boils down to the correct use of two of the smallest things in your house, the on-off knob on your set and the simple yet powerful word *No*. Now, don't look around for much support. You'll have to hammer out your own philosophy. One that fits you and your family. But, for sure, do something soon. Let's take seriously these words:

> Fix your thoughts on what is true and good and right. Think about things that are pure and lovely, and dwell on the fine, good things in others.
> —Paul, to twentieth century Christians
> (Philippians 4:8, TLB)

Believe me, the ultimate benefits you'll enjoy will be worth much more than $500 and they will certainly last a lot longer.

For a change, unplug the plug-in drug.

Deepening Your Roots
Psalm 25:15; Ezekiel 20:21–31; 1 John 2:15–17

Branching Out
1. I challenge you to turn your TV off for one entire week and fill those free hours with at least one good book, listening to some new music, playing a game, taking a walk, visiting with someone you've not seen in over three months.
2. For every hour of TV you watch, spend the same amount of time reading a book.

Please Be Careful

The package arrived safely. Somebody was thoughtful to remember to stick an important reminder on it when it was mailed. Oh, it had a few scuff marks and a bent corner or two, but by and large, nothing was damaged. Actually, it wasn't that expensive . . . just a photo of my family sandwiched between two flats of cardboard. Just a picture of six people with the same last name, four of whom were delivered by God into our home between 1961 and 1970. The reminder on the package jumped out at me:

FRAGILE: HANDLE WITH CARE

We've tried to do that. Like all other parents, there have been times of exasperation and exhaustion, frustration and failure, but deep down inside we have tried not to forget just how fragile these individually prepared arrows in our quiver really are.

Their mother and I realized this anew recently as we gulped and groaned our way through a televised presentation on child abuse. We choked back the tears as we heard and watched two hours of grim realism, more shocking and depressing than any make-believe horror

34

movie director could ever devise. You better sit down before you read these factual statistics. Take a deep breath.

- Two hundred thousand children are physically abused each year.
- Of those, between 60,000 and 100,000 are *sexually* abused.
- Fifteen to twenty percent of American families abuse their children.
- Two thirds of all child abuse occurs with children under four years of age . . . one-third are *under six months*.
- The number one killer of children under five years of age is child abuse.
- Four thousand children die annually because of child abuse. It is estimated that, including the *unreported* abuses, the number could be as high as 50,000.
- Child-abusers are found in every category of our society. No social or economic or religious types are excluded.

No, most child-abuers are not mentally deficient. Only ten percent are classified "mentally disturbed." The rest are people who appear to be very normal; they just "cannot cope." Maybe *you're* in the ninety-percent category. You can get help through counselors and public agencies. Please do. You'll be treated with professional and personal care, I am told. For the sake of your child, please do.

But maybe all you need is a little encouragement, a few well-worded reminders to "handle with care" those little people who may seem to be anything but fragile. I think if we would let them talk, here's what they would say:

- My hands are small; please don't expect perfection whenever I make my bed, draw a picture, or throw a ball. My legs are short; please slow down so I can keep up with you.
- My eyes have not seen the world as yours have; please let me explore safely. Don't restrict me unnecessarily.
- Housework will always be there. I'm only little for a short time—please take time to explain things to me about this wonderful world, and do so willingly.
- My feelings are tender; please be sensitive to my needs. Don't nag me all day long . . . treat me as you would like to be treated.
- I am a special gift from God; please treasure me as God intended you to do, holding me accountable for my actions, giving me guidelines to live by, and disciplining me in a loving manner.
- I need your encouragement to grow. Please go easy on the criticism; remember you can criticize the things I do without criticizing me.
- Please give me the freedom to make decisions concerning myself. Permit me to fail, so that I can learn from my mistakes. Then someday I'll be prepared to make the kind of decisions life requires of me.
- Please don't do things over for me. Somehow that makes me feel that my efforts didn't quite measure up to your expectations. I know it's hard, but please don't try to compare me with my brother or my sister.
- Please don't be afraid to leave for a weekend together. Kids need vacations from parents, just as parents need vacations from kids. Besides, it's a great way to show us kids that your marriage is very special.

Because they are fragile, handling children with care is essential. You'll be glad you did when all you have is an old photo and the memory of a package God delivered into your care many, many years ago.

Deepening Your Roots
1 Kings 3:16–27; Psalm 127:1–5; Proverbs 17:6; Luke 18:15–17

Branching Out
1. Set aside one hour a day this week and play with your children or grandchildren. Do whatever *they* desire to do. Let them tell/show you what fun is all about.
2. Do something special with each of your (or a friend's) children this week. Don't do it as a group; give each one a special time to be alone with you.
3. Take a picture of your (or a friend's) children this week and when developed frame it. Write on the back of the photo: Fragile—Handle with Care.

Resentment

Leonard Holt was a paragon of respectability. He was a middle-aged, hard-working lab technician who had worked at the same Pennsylvania paper mill for nineteen years. Having been a Boy Scout leader, an affectionate father, a member of the local fire brigade, and a regular church-goer, he was admired as a model in his community. Until . . .

. . . that image exploded in a well-planned hour of bloodshed one brisk October morning. Holt decided to mount a one-man revolt against the world he inwardly resented. A proficient marksman, he stuffed two pistols into his coat pockets—a .45 automatic and a Smith and Wesson .38—before he drove his station wagon to the mill. Parking quietly, he gripped a gun in each fist, then slowly stalked into the shop. He started shooting with such calculated frenzy that it resembled a scene out of "Gunsmoke." He filled several of his fellow workmen with two and three bullets apiece, firing more than thirty shots in all . . . deliberately killing some of the men he had known for over fifteen years. When a posse was formed to capture the man, they found him standing in his doorway, snarling defiantly:

"Come and get me, you—; I'm not taking any more of your—."

Total bewilderment swept over the neighborhood. Puzzled policemen and friends finally discovered a tenuous chain of logic behind his brief reign of terror. Down deep within the heart and soul of Leonard Holt rumbled intense resentment. The man who had appeared like a monk on the outside was seething with murderous hatred within. A subsequent investigation led officials to numerous discoveries yielding such evidence. Several of the victims had been promoted over him while he remained in the same position. More than one in his car pool had quit riding with him due to his reckless driving. A neighbor had been threatened, then struck by Holt after an argument over a fallen tree. The man was *brimming* with resentful rage that could be held in check no longer.

Beneath his picture in *Time* magazine, the caption told the truth:

RESPONSIBLE, RESPECTABLE—AND RESENTFUL.

So it is with resentment. Allowed to fester through neglect, the toxic fumes of hatred foam to a boil within the steamroom of the soul. Pressure mounts to a maddening magnitude. By then it's only a matter of time. The damage is always tragic, often irreparable:

- a battered child
- a crime of passion
- ugly, caustic words
- loss of a job

- a runaway
- a bad record
- domestic disharmony
- a ruined testimony

None of this is new. Solomon described the problem long ago:

> Pretty words may hide a wicked heart, just as a pretty glaze covers a common clay pot.
>
> A man with hate in his heart may sound pleasant enough, but don't believe him; for he is cursing you in his heart. Though he pretends to be so kind, his hatred will finally come to light for all to see (Proverbs 26:23–26 TLB).

The answer to resentment isn't complicated, it's just painful. It requires *honesty*. You must first admit it's there. It then requires *humility*. You must confess it before the One who died for such sins. It may even be necessary for you to make it right with those you have offended out of resentful bitterness. Finally, it requires *vulnerability*—a willingness to keep that tendency submissive to God's regular reproof, and a genuinely teachable, unguarded attitude.

Nobody ever dreamed Leonard Holt had a problem with resentment. And nobody dreams *you* do either.

Not yet . . .

Deepening Your Roots
2 Timothy 2:24; Hebrews 12:14 and 15; James 3:14–16; 1
   John 2:9–11

Branching Out
1. Be honest. What's a resentment you harbor inside yourself?
2. Talk to a fellow worker, a friend, or your spouse and
   quietly probe to see if there is any problem between the
   two of you.
3. Would people be surprised if they knew your inner
   thoughts? Are some of those thoughts ''resentment''?

Health

To set the record straight, I am neither a doctor nor the son of a doctor, and since I may *sound* like a doctor, you must not be misled. What I have to share comes not from intensive medical training but from extensive practical thinking. Because I am not qualified to write a prescription, hoping you'll take the medicine, I will write a philosophy, hoping you'll take the message.

Frank Burgess, the American humorist, told the truth when he said,

"Our bodies are apt to be our autobiographies."

Arthur Schopenhauer, the astute German philosopher, put it another way:

The greatest mistake a man can make is to sacrifice health for any other advantage.

Health is the thing that makes you feel that *now* is the best time of the year. Next to having a good conscience, health is to be valued most. But it isn't! Of all the good and perfect gifts God grants us, it is the least recognized. We either ignore it (like a bad habit) or we take advantage of it (like a good wife). Health is the stepchild of our lives. Mistreated and misunderstood,

42

it exists without encouragement and serves us without reward. Occasionally, it is like the timid student in school who raises her hand for help but finds the teacher too busy to notice or too demanding to care. But there are also times when health loses its cool and refuses to stay silent any longer. Its frustrations reach such a fevered pitch that it screams for our attention . . . and it gets it!

Many of us are notoriously negligent when it comes to maintaining good health. Take *rest*, for example. Written across our minds is the statement made famous by some so-called dedicated saint:

"I'd rather burn out than rust out!"

What kind of a choice is that? Either way, you're "out." That's like saying, "I'd rather die while skiing than while sleeping." Whichever the choice, you're a cold corpse. Good health depends upon proper rest. Compromising here is just plain carnal! It is no better than gossip or stealing or murder. Rest can be as spiritual as hours in prayer—*maybe more*.

Take *food*, for example. Your body and mine cannot be better than the food used each day to nourish, strengthen, and rebuild it—no matter how much we love the Lord! God never intended that we function on a constant diet of imitation or refined foods, devoid of nutrition and inundated with preservatives . . . raised in fields polluted with insecticides and other poisons. You may be a Bible teacher, gifted, and in great demand—but if you cram only junk down the throat, your health will go down the tube. Good food (and the right amount) can be as spiritual as teaching the truth—*sometimes more*.

Exercise is yet another example. No amount of witnessing or worship can substitute for regular physical exercise. Every cell and organ of the old "bod" tends to increase in efficiency through exercise. Vigorous exercise stimulates the mind, the blood, the muscles, the senses. It even affects our worries by flushing them out as we perspire in recreation and an active change of pace. It's no surprise to me that the very first preparation suggested by Dr. Laurence J. Peter on "How to make things go right" is: REVITALIZE YOUR BODY. Exercise can be as spiritual as attending a church service—*perhaps more*.

Three questions: How are we to glorify God? Where is the temple of the Holy Spirit? What is to be presented to the Lord as a living sacrifice?

One answer: The body. Let's not think that loud prayers and lengthy Bible studies and lovely church services will cause God to smile at lousy health habits.

Keep your balance. It's a long drop from the thin wire of fanaticism to the hard floor of realism . . . and the sudden stop never helps anybody.

Deepening Your Roots
Proverbs 23:20 and 21; Daniel 1:8–16; 1 Corinthians 6:12–19

Branching Out
1. If you are overweight and unable to shake off those pounds, then seek help—even if it costs. Or, if you've been putting off dropping those excess pounds, decide today to lose—amount by—, and do it!
2. Choose three items from the list below and stop eating them for one month. See if you feel better by that time. Absolutely no cheating. Reward yourself in thirty days if you did this assignment.

chocolate	coffee	candy	cookies
ice cream	cake	pop	pie

3. Take up some sport or exercise program and do it consistently (three to five times a week) for one month. Write down how you feel today and then how you feel in one month.

Isolation and Involvement

Elevators are weird places, aren't they? Especially crowded ones.

You're crammed in close with folks you've never met, so you try really hard not to touch them. And nobody talks, either. The one thing you may hear is an occasional "Out, please" or "Oh, I'm sorry" as somebody clumsily steps on someone's toe. You don't look at anyone; in fact, you don't look anywhere but up, watching those dumb numbers go on and off. Strange. People who are all about the same height and speak the same language are suddenly as silent as a roomful of nuns when they occupy common space.

It's almost as if there's an official sign that reads:

NO TALKING, NO SMILING, NO TOUCHING,
AND NO EYE CONTACT ALLOWED WITHOUT
WRITTEN CONSENT OF THE MANAGEMENT.
NO EXCEPTIONS!!

Years ago I was speaking on the campus of the University of Oklahoma. After the meeting, a crazy group of three or four guys invited me to have a Coke with them. Since we were several floors up in the student

46

center, we decided to take the elevator down. As the door slid open, the thing was full of people who gave us that hey-you-guys-aren't-gonna-try-to-get-in-are-you? look. But we did, naturally. I was last. There wasn't even room to turn around. I felt the door close against my back as everyone stared in my direction. I smiled big and said loudly, "You might have wondered why we called this meeting today!" The place broke open with laughter. It was the most amazing thing to watch . . . people actually *talking,* actually *relating* to each other . . . *on an elevator.*

I've been thinking lately that an elevator is a microcosm of our world today: a large, impersonal institution where anonymity, isolation, and independence are the uniform of the day. A basic quality of our healthy social lives is being diluted, distorted, and demeaned by the "elevator mentality." We are way out of balance in the area of relating to people.

A recently published report by Ralph Larkin, a sociologist, on the crises facing suburban youth, underscores several aspects of this new malaise of the spirit. Many children of American affluence are depicted as passively accepting a way of life they view as empty and meaningless. A syndrome is now set in motion that includes "a low threshold of boredom, a constricted expression of emotions, and an apparent absence of joy in anything that is not immediately consumable."[5] Makes sense when you observe the significant role now played by music, drugs, booze, sex, and status-symbol possessions. Take away rock concerts and sports events and you seldom witness much display of strong emotion.

Exit: Involvement and motivation. Enter: Indifference, noncommitment, disengagement, no sharing or caring . . . meals eaten with hi-fi headsets turned up loud, even separate bedrooms, each with a personal telephone, TV and turntable, private toilet, and an it's-none-of-your-business attitude. No hassles . . . no conflicts . . . no accountability. No need to share. Or reach out. Or give a rip. Just watch the numbers and look at nobody.

Dr. Philip Zimbardo, a professor of psychology at Stanford and author of one of the most widely used textbooks in the field, addresses this issue in a *Psychology Today* article entitled "The Age of Indifference." He pulls no punches as he writes:

I know of no more potent killer than isolation. There is no more destructive influence on physical and mental health than the isolation of you from me and of us from them. It has been shown to be a central agent in the etiology of depression, paranoia, schizophrenia, rape, suicide, mass murder . . .

And then he adds:

The devil's strategy for our times is to trivialize human existence in a number of ways: by isolating us from one another while creating the delusion that the reasons are time pressures, work demands, or anxieties created by economic uncertainty; by fostering narcissism and the fierce competition to be No. 1 . . . [6]

Ouch!

We must come to terms with all this. We must come down hard on it . . . the need is *urgent!*

Our Savior modeled the answer perfectly. He didn't just preach it. He cared. He listened. He served. He reached out. He supported. He affirmed and encouraged. He stayed in touch. He walked with people . . . never took the elevator.

The only escape from indifference is to think of people as our most cherished resource. We need to work hard at re-establishing family fun, meaningful mealtimes, people involvement, evenings *without* the television blaring, nonsuperficial conversations, times when we genuinely get involved with folks in need—not *just* pray for them.

Stop the elevator. I want to get off.

Deepening Your Roots
Proverbs 18:1; Mark 2:13–17; Luke 14:12–23; Acts 6:1–4; Revelation 19:7–9

Branching Out
1. Next time you're on an elevator, break the ice and talk to a stranger.
2. Set aside an evening this week when you either invite someone over, or take the initiative and visit someone who you know tends to stay at home and away from people.
3. Decide on something you normally always do "alone" (eat lunch by yourself, grocery shop, take a walk, etc.) and find someone to join you.

"The Opra Ain't Over"

The words were painted in bright red on a banner hung over the wall near the forty-yard line of Texas Stadium, home of the Dallas Cowboys football team, on Sunday afternoon.

The guys in silver and blue were struggling to stay in the race for the playoffs. So a dyed-in-the-wool Cowboy fan decided he would offer some back-home encouragement straight out of his country-western repertoire. He scratched around his garage on Saturday and found some paint, a big brush, and a ruler . . . then splashed those words on a king-sized bed sheet for all America to read:

THE OPRA AIN'T OVER
'TIL THE FAT LADY SINGS.

It was his way of saying, "We're hanging in there. Don't count us out. We have three games left before anybody can say for sure . . . so we're not givin' up! The opra ain't over."

Sure is easy to jump to conclusions, isn't it? People who study trends make it their business to manufacture out of their imaginations the proposed (and "inevitable'') end result. Pollsters do that, too. After a sampling of three percent of our country, vast and stunning stats are predicted. Our worry increases. We are all informed that so-and-so will, *for sure*, wind up doing such-and-such. At times it's downright scary. And discouraging.

Every once in awhile it's helpful to remember times when those folks wound up with egg on their faces. Much to our amazement, the incredible often happens.

- Like when Wellington whipped Napoleon
- Or Truman beat Dewey
- And Washington won in the Rose Bowl
- Like that time the earthquake didn't hit
- And England *didn't* surrender
- And *Star Wars* didn't grab a fistful of Academy Awards
- And Hitler *wasn't* the anti-Christ
- And the communists *didn't* take over America by 1980
- And Muhammad Ali *could* get beaten
- And a nation *could* continue on through the disillusionments of Vietnam, White House and senatorial scandals, assassination attempts, energy crises, nuclear mishaps, and economic recessions.

Yes, at many a turn we have been tempted to jump to so-called ''obvious'' conclusions, only to be surprised by a strange curve thrown our way. God is good at that. When He does, it really encourages His people.

Can you recall a few biblical examples?

- A wiry teenager, armed with only a sling and a stone, whipped a giant over nine feet tall. Nobody would've predicted that.
- With an Egyptian army fast approaching and no possible way to escape, all looked bleak. But not so!

Against nature and reversing the pull of gravity, a sea opened up and allowed the Hebrews to walk across.

- And how about the vast, "indestructible" wall around Jericho? Who would've imagined?
- Or that dead-end street at Golgotha miraculously opening back up at an empty tomb three days later?
- Or a handful of very human disciples turning the world upside down?

Anybody—and I mean anybody—who would have been near enough to have witnessed any one of those predicaments would certainly have said, "Curtains . . . the opra is over!"

A lot of you who read this page are backed up against a set of circumstances that seem to spell T-H-E E-N-D. All looks almost hopeless. Pretty well finished. Apparently over. Maybe you need to read that again, underlining those words:

seem to . . . almost . . . pretty well . . . apparently.

Your adversary would love for you to assume the worst. He'd enjoy seeing you heave a sigh and resign yourself to depressed feelings that accompany defeat, failure, maximum resentment, and minimum faith. After all, it's fairly obvious you're through. Well . . . since when does "fairly obvious" draw the curtain on the last act? It's been my experience that when God is involved, *anything* can happen. The One who directed that stone in between Goliath's eyes and split the Red Sea down the middle and leveled that wall around Jericho and brought His Son back from beyond takes a delight in mixing up the odds as He alters the obvious and bypasses the inevitable.

The blind songwriter, Fanny Crosby, put it another way:

Chords that were broken will vibrate once more.

In other words, don't manufacture conclusions. Don't even think in terms of "this is the way things will turn out." Be open. Stay that way. God has a beautiful way of bringing good vibrations out of broken chords. When the Lord is in it, anything is possible. In His performances there are dozens of "fat ladies" waiting to sing the finale.

The opra ain't over.

Deepening Your Roots
James 4:13–17; Proverbs 19:21; Matthew 19:26; Genesis 15:2–4, 16:1–4, 21:1–7

Branching Out
1. What's something you've jumped to conclusions about?
2. Write down how you think your day will turn out. At today's end, note what really took place:
3. What's a circumstance you're facing that appears to spell THE END? Pray about it now and ask God to teach you in this situation the principle from today's thought.

Presumption

There is a very delicate line between faith and presumption. On the surface both appear daring, courageous, and impressive. Underneath, however, one is met with God's approval while the other incites His wrath and prompts His judgment.

Let's think about this word, presumption, for a few moments. Actually, it is a combination of two English terms: *pre* meaning "in front of, before, ahead" and *assume* meaning "to take upon oneself, to take over." Mixing that together we come up with the idea of running ahead and taking over, the act of taking something beforehand. Webster suggests that when one presumes, one "takes upon oneself without leave or warrant," one "goes beyond what is right or proper, overstepping due bounds, taking unwarranted liberties."

Excerpts from the following article from yesterday's newspaper regarding a church service in Newport, Tennessee, illustrates presumption:

TWO PREACHERS DIE IN TEST OF FAITH

Two . . . preachers who had survived the bites of poisonous snakes tested their faith with strychnine and died . . . a few hours after drinking the poison. . . .

54

Cocke County officers said copperheads and rattlesnakes were handled at the mountain sect's religious service Saturday night.

After the snakes had been handled, Mr. Williams and Mr. Pack drank the strychnine as a further test of their faith.

Both preachers had survived snakebites at previous religious services.

I must confess that upon reading that article, I immediately took issue with the repeated statement that this was a "test of their faith." No, in my opinion, that wasn't faith, it was *presumption*. They took upon themselves certain liberties that were unwarranted . . . they overstepped their proper bounds . . . they therefore incurred God's judgment, not His favor. As the congregation was oohing and ahhing, God's heart was breaking. Their act was a circus-like display of the flesh designed to attract attention. The shadow of the Almighty did not rest upon it. As with Saul, who flaunted his role and presumed upon the priesthood (1 Samuel 13), death finally came and censured the arrogant act. Leprosy fell upon Uzziah for a similar deed according to 2 Chronicles 26:16–21 (please read).

Not all presumptuous acts are as notorious as these I have mentioned. Sometimes when we are determined to have our own way—especially when we are restless, tired of waiting, anxious for action—we run ahead and then salve our conscience by calling our decision "faith." I believe that this is what David had in mind when he wrote Psalm 19:12–13:

Who can discern his errors? Acquit me of hidden faults.
Also keep back Thy servant from presumptuous sins; Let
them not rule over me . . .

Because we are not aware of our "hidden faults,"
we need divine assistance and acquittal. We are prone
to rush on, refusing to be patient and to quietly wait for
God's time. This tendency toward "presumptuous sins"
is ever with us. David asked that God might keep him
back—hold him, restrain him—from presumptuous sins.
He added, "Let them not rule over me." That seems
to suggest that presumption can dominate a person's
life. Once we fall into the habit, we can presume upon
God without even realizing we are doing so. We can
believe in our hearts that our actions are humble steps
of faith when all the while they are as presumptuous as
handling snakes and drinking poison, though not nearly
so sensational.

Admittedly, it is often difficult to know the difference
between faith and presumption. That is all the more
reason to pray as David prayed, "Keep back thy servant . . . " How pleasing it must be to God to hear us
genuinely say, "Hold me back . . . I'm willing to
wait . . . I want *Your* will most of all, my Father."

Are you waiting for His leading today? Good for you!
If the light is red or even yellow, you're wise to let Him
hold you back. When it turns green, you'll know it.
Don't race your motor while you're waiting. You'll burn
up all your fuel . . . and you might slip across that delicate line. God's moving-violation fines are quite expensive. Ask the congregation in Newport, Tennessee.

Deepening Your Roots

Numbers 14:41–45; 1 Corinthians 10:9–11; 2 Chronicles 26:16–21

Branching Out

1. In the habit of rushing ahead of God? Name one area or thing you're not willing to wait on God for. Now, be like David and ask God to hold you back and keep you from moving ahead of Him.
2. Force yourself to wait an extra twenty-four hours before making a decision today that you felt must be decided on by this afternoon or evening.
3. Name a matter that you tend to deal with in your own way and time. How about letting God in on the situation?

Designer-label Planet

With the help of a telescope or a microscope we are ushered immediately into a world of incredible, infinite design. Take your choice: planets or paramecia . . . astronomy or biology . . . "the infinite meadows of heaven" (Longfellow) or the diminutive microbes of earth—and sheer, unemotional intelligence will *force* you to mumble to yourself, "Behind all this was more than chance. This design is the result of a designer!" His name? God, the Creator.

To deny that these worlds beyond the lens are the results of God's design is to defy all mathematical calculations of chance. Let me prove that by borrowing the following illustration from a noted scientist and former president of the New York Academy of Sciences, Dr. A. Cressy Morrison. Suppose I would take ten pennies and mark them from 1 to 10 and give them to you to put into your pocket. I'd ask you to give them a good shake, then I'd say, "I'm going to reach into your pocket and draw out penny number 1." My chance of doing this would be 1 in 10 . . . and you would be surprised if I accomplished it. Now, let's go further. I would put number 1 back into your pocket, have you shake them again, and I'd say, "I will now draw out number 2."

My chances are much slimmer—1 in 100. If I were to draw out number 3 in the same way, the chance would be 1 in 1000. If I draw out each number in order, following the identical process, the ultimate chance factor would reach the unbelievable figure of 1 chance in 10 billion!

If I performed that act before your eyes you would probably say, ''The game is fixed.'' That's exactly what I am saying about the galaxies and the germs—and, more important, your life and mine on this earth. The arrangement *is* fixed . . . there is a Designer—God—and He is not silent. As a matter of fact, He declares His presence twenty-four hours a day. How? Listen to Psalm 19:1–4 (TLB):

> The heavens are telling the glory of God; they are a marvelous display of His craftsmanship. Day and night they keep on telling about God. Without a sound or word, silent in the skies, their message reaches out to all the world. The sun lives in the heavens where God placed it. . . .

Let's think about that. Let's remind ourselves of a few fundamental, proven facts of science we learned in high school. It is amazing how they dovetail with Psalm 19.

1. Temperature. The sun is 12,000 degrees Fahrenheit. All of earth's heat is from the sun. We are 93 million miles away—just the right distance, I might add. If the earth's temperature were an *average* of 50 degrees hotter or colder, all life on this planet would cease to exist. Why is the sun 12,000 degrees hot? Why not 1200

degrees . . . or 120,000 . . . or24,000? Why was the earth fixed at *exactly* the right distance away so that we could have a pleasant 70 degrees temperature this morning? Why not twice as far, twice as close . . . or 1000 times as far? Answer: because all life would perish. Was this delicately chosen to meet the requirements of the living cell . . . or by chance?

2. Rotation. This planet rotates 365 times each year as it passes around the sun. Suppose it rotated 36 times instead? Well, our days and nights would be ten times as long—we'd be terribly hot on one side and unbearable cold on the other . . . and life would begin to disappear. By chance?

3. Air. Let's limit our thoughts to one element of air—oxygen. This ingredient constitutes about 21 percent of our atmosphere. Why 21 percent? Why not 4 percent or 10 percent . . . or, for that matter, *50 percent?* Well, if 50 percent, the first time someone lit a match we'd *all* be on fire. Is 21 percent by chance?

What's my point? This planet was designed by God so that it would support one thing: life. Without life, earth would be another planetary wasteland. It would be like a wedding without a bride . . . a car without gears and wheels. Why life? Because only through life can matter understand God and glorify its Maker! Only through faith in the Lord Jesus Christ can the designed know and glorify the Designer.

Deepening Your Roots
Psalm 33:6–22; 65; 104

Branching Out
1. Look in the newspaper or a magazine and find some other scientific data which could also illustrate today's thought.
2. Watch an educational TV program today that teaches you something new about science.

Growing Old

Growing old, like taxes, is a fact we all must face. Now, you're not going to get me to declare when growing *up* stops and growing *old* starts—not on your life! But there are some signs we can read along life's journey that suggest we are entering the transition (how's that for diplomacy?).

Physically, the aging "bod" puts on the brakes. You begin to huff and puff when you used to rip and zip. You prefer to sit more than stand . . . to watch more than to do . . . to forget your birthday rather than remember it! *Mentally*, the aging brain longs for relief. You can't remember like you used to, and you don't respond like you ought to. You start thinking more about yesterday and tomorrow and less about today. *Emotionally*, you undergo strange fears and feelings you once swore would "never occur in me," such as:

- Being negative, critical, and downright ornery at times.
- Being reluctant to let those who are younger carry more responsibility.
- Feeling unwanted and "in the way."
- Preoccupied with "what if" rather frequently.
- Feeling guilty over previous mistakes and wrong decisions.

- Feeling forgotten, unloved, lonely, and passed by.
- Threatened by sounds, speed, financial uncertainty, and disease.
- Resisting the need to adjust and adapt.

All this—and there is much more—is worsened by the memory of those days when you once were so very efficient, capable, needed, and fulfilled. As you look into the mirror, you're forced to admit that the fingers of age have begun to scratch their marks upon your house of clay . . . and it's hard to believe your twilight years could be of any worth.

How wrong! How terribly wrong! How destructive such thoughts can be! How quickly such thinking can sentence you to the prison cell of self-pity, surrounded by the four bleak walls of doubt, depression, uselessness, and grief.

God's patriarchs have always been among His choicest possessions. Abraham was far more effective once he grew old and mellow. Moses wasn't used with any measure of success until he turned eighty. Caleb was eighty-five when he began to enjoy God's best goals. Samuel was old, old when the God of Israel led him to establish the "school of the prophets," an institution that had a lasting influence for spirituality and godliness in the centuries to come. And who could deny the way God used Paul during his last days on his knees, writing words of encouragement in letters we cherish today!

No one fails to see that growing old has its difficulties and heartaches. It does, indeed. But to see only the hot sands of your desert experience and miss the lovely oases here and there (though they may be few) is to turn the latter part of your journey through life into an arid, tasteless endurance which makes everyone miserable.

Please don't forget—God has decided to let you live this long. Your old age is not a mistake . . . nor an oversight . . . nor an afterthought. Isn't it about time you cooled your tongue and softened your smile with a refreshing drink from the water of God's oasis? You've been thirsty a long, long time.

Deepening Your Roots
Proverbs 16:31; Psalm 92:14; Isaiah 46:4; Titus 2:2–3

Branching Out
1. Spend time with an elderly person and find out some of his fondest memories, and in what ways God has used him, or he hopes God will use him.
2. Begin praying about your future, that you will be a faithful and valuable vessel.
2. Ask this question of three elderly people whom you consider to be godly: What would you do over or do differently to develop a closer relationship with God? Heed their words.

Reality

I arrived at my office unusually early this morning. Things were quiet, the sky was heavy and overcast, a normal California fall morning. My mind was on my schedule as I fumbled with the keys. In standard Swindoll fashion I pushed the door wide open in a hurry—only to be stopped dead in my tracks. A chill went up my back as I peered into the spooky study. The light switch is across the room, so I stood there at the door staring at the most startling reminder of reality imaginable! In the middle of the floor, sitting on rollers, was a *casket* . . . with a wilted spray of flowers on top alongside a picture of ME! Now, my friend, is you want to know how to awaken someone from early morning slumber, *this routine will surely do it!* I suppose I stood there five minutes without moving a muscle as I blinked and gathered my senses. I checked my watch and was pleased to see the second hand still moving. All my reflexes responded correctly and my breath still brought a patch of fog to the mirror. "Praise God," I thought, "I'm still here."

But the fact is, I won't always be. That's reality. The practical joker taught me an unforgettable lesson. Some future day, some quiet, heavily overcast morning, the sun will rise again on this earth, but that day I will be gone . . . absent from this body. Dust will settle on these books I love . . . another will have the keys I now carry . . . and answer this phone . . . and fill this room with his voice and laughter and tears. That's reality. Painful and difficult as it may be to tolerate such thoughts—that's fact, that's real!

It was in 1935 that Thomas Stearns Eliot wrote:

Human kind cannot bear very much reality.

Thirty years later the old British poet and his loved ones were forced to bear it. He stopped writing . . . and breathing.

Reality, though difficult, is dependable. It always keeps its word, though its word may be hard to bear.

I would much prefer to live my life on the sharp, cutting edge of reality than dreaming on the soft, phony mattress of fantasy. Reality is the tempered poker that keeps the fires alive . . . it's the spark that prompts the engine to keep running . . . the hard set of facts that refuses to let feeling overrule logic. It's reality that forces every Alice out of her Wonderland and into God's wonderful plan. Its undaunted determination has pulled many a wanderer, lost in the maze of meanderings, back to the real world of right and wrong, the false and the true. Reality, I remind you, is the world from which most every emotionally—and mentally—disturbed patient has escaped—and the point to which they must return before health is restored. Hard as it may be to bear, it brings a practical security second to none. It is, unquestionably, the healthiest place on earth.

It was Jesus' realistic view of the Pharisees that exposed the sackcloth of hypocrisy beneath their religious robes (Matthew 23). It was His realistic attitude toward the devil that resulted in Satan's departing from Him (Matthew 4:1–11). It was reality that enabled Him to perform spiritual heart surgery on the woman at the well (John 4) . . . and to stand uncondemningly beside the adulteress (John 8) . . . and to pray as He did the night of His arrest (John 17). Reality, in fact, was part of His motive in bearing the cross for you and me.

While our entire world is sinking in the quagmire of human opinions, theories, philosophies, and dreams, our Lord invites us to stand firmly on the rock of reality. And what does the realistic mind-set include? Well, these are eternally etched in the granite of God's Book. They include such things as:

- Man is a depraved sinner, terribly in need.
- Our only hope is in Jesus Christ—His death and resurrection.
- Receiving Him brings instant forgiveness and eternal grace.
- Death is certain but not the end.
- Heaven is a real place.
- So is hell.
- We cannot escape standing before Him.
- The time to prepare is NOW.

Some quiet, heavily overcast morning you and I will be *forced* to face reality. The second hand on our inner watch will suddenly stop. Time will be no more. At that moment—even before your casket is ordered—your passport will be clutched in your hand. What will it read? "REDEEMED" or "CONDEMNED"? Face it, man—that's reality! And *that day* it won't be a joke. That day you won't be reading this—you'll be experiencing *that*.

Deepening Your Roots
Job 19:25–27; 1 Corinthians 15:1–58; Colossians 2:17

Branching Out
19 Write down on a 3x5 card the list from today's reading (things included in the granite of God's Book—Man is a depraver sinner . . . , Our only hope . . . , etc.). Put this card by your phone to read often this week and to remind you of the reality of God's words.

2. Play detective this week as you're viewing the tube: watch for one very realistic commercial, and one that's totally *un*realistic.

Lifelines

I'm writing these words on my forty-second birthday.

No big deal . . . just another stabbing realization that I'm not getting any younger. I know that because the cake won't hold all the candles. Even if it could the frosting would melt before I'd be able to blow all of them out. My kind and thoughtful secretary reminded me of another approach I could take. She gave me a birthday card showing an old guy standing beside a cake *covered* with candles. On the front it reads:

Don't feel you're getting old if you can't blow out all the candles . . .

And inside:

. . . just BEAT 'em out with your cane.

Children are about as encouraging. In all seriousness my youngest asked me recently if they had *catsup* when I was a boy. I tried not to look offended—he could have asked if they had the wheel. But I was pleased to inform him that we not only had catsup . . . but also electricity, talking movies, the radio, cars, and indoor plumbing. He seemed amazed as he gave me that you-gotta-bekidding-look, then turned and walked away. I suddenly felt the need to lie down and take a nap.

But birthdays are milestones . . . significant points in the passing of time . . . specific yet mute reminders that more sand has passed through the hour glass. They do, however, give us a handle on the measurement of time which, when you boil it down into minutes, really moves along at a pretty good clip. There are 60 of them every hour . . . 1,440 every day . . . over 10 thousand of them each week . . . about 525 thousand per year. As of today—I've experienced over 22 million of them. Talk about feeling old!

But they pass so quietly, so consistently, they fool you. That's part of the reason C.S. Lewis used to say:

> The safest road to hell is the gradual one—the gentle slope, soft underfoot, without sudden turnings, without milestones, without signposts. The long, dull, monotonous years of middle-aged prosperity or adversity are excellent campaigning weather for the devil.

We mark our calendars with *deadlines*—dates that set limits for the completion of objectives and projects. To ignore those deadlines brings consequences. To live without deadlines is to live an inefficient, unorganized life, drifting with the breeze of impulse on the fickle wave of moods. We set deadlines because they help us accomplish the essentials . . . they discipline our use of time . . . they measure the length of our leash on the clothesline of demands.

God, however, brings about birthdays . . . not as deadlines but *lifelines*. He builds them into our calendar once every year to enable us to make an annual appraisal, not only of our length of life but our depth. Not simply to tell us we're growing older . . . but to help us determine if we are also growing deeper. These lifelines are not like that insurance policy you invested in last year. There's no automatic promise of annual renewal. Obviously, if God has given you another year to live for Him, He has some things in mind . . . He has some very special plans to pull off through your life. Surely it includes more than existing 1,440 minutes a day!

The psalmist gives us the perfect prayer to pray every year our lifeline rolls around.

> So teach us to number our days, that we may present to Thee a heart of wisdom (Psalm 90:12).

Now let me caution you. Don't expect wisdom to come into your life like great chunks of rock on a conveyor belt. It isn't like that. It's not splashy and bold . . . nor is it dispensed like a prescription across a counter. Wisdom comes privately from God as a by-product of right decisions, godly reactions, and the application of scriptural principles to daily circumstances. Wisdom comes, for example, not from seeking after a ministry . . . but more from anticipating the fruit of a disciplined life. Not from trying to do great things for God . . . but more from being faithful to the small, obscure tasks few people ever see.

Stop and reflect. Are you just growing *old* . . . or are you also growing *up*? As you ''number your days'' do you count just years—the grinding measurement of minutes—or can you find marks of wisdom . . . character traits that were not there when you were younger?

Take a look. You really don't have a lot longer, you know. As a matter of fact, one of these years your lifeline will be God's deadline.

Deepening Your Roots
Proverbs 4:1–19; Job 12:10–13; Proverbs 16:31

Branching Out
1. List ten ways you've grown deeper in the last decade.
2. Identify three areas of your life that you'd like to see changed in the coming decade. Choose the most important to you. Decide on three things you could do to make your wish come true. Begin doing one of those today.

Adversity and Prosperity

There are two extreme tests that disturb our balance in life. Each has its own set of problems. On one side is *adversity*. Solomon realized this when he wrote:

> If you faint in the day of adversity, your strength is small (Proverbs 24:10, RSV).

The *Good News Bible* paraphrases that verse:

> If you are weak in a crisis, you are weak indeed.

Adversity is a good test of our resiliency, our ability to cope, to stand back up, to recover from misfortune. Adversity is a painful pedagogue.

On the other side is *prosperity*. In all honesty, it's a tougher test than adversity. The Scottish essayist and historian, Thomas Carlyel, agreed when he said:

> Adversity is sometimes hard upon a man; but for one man who can stand prosperity, there are a hundred that will stand adversity.[7]

Precious few are those who can live in the lap of luxury . . . who can keep their moral, spiritual, and financial equilibrium . . . while balancing on the elevated tightrope of success. It's ironic that most of us can handle a sudden demotion much better than a sizable promotion.

Why?

Well, it really isn't too difficult to explain. When adversity strikes, life becomes rather simple. Our need is to survive. But when prosperity occurs, life gets complicated. And our needs are numerous, often extremely complex. Invariably, our integrity is put to the test. And there is about one in a hundred who can dance to the tune of success without paying the piper named Compromise.

Now, before we get too carried away, let's understand that being successful isn't necessarily wrong. Being promoted, being elevated to a place of prominence can come from God Himself.

> For not from the east, nor from the west,
> Nor from the desert comes exaltation;
> But God is the judge;
> He puts down one, and exalts another (Psalm 75:6–7).

Asaph, the guy who wrote those words, was correct. It is the Lord's sovereign right to demote as well as to promote . . . and we seldom know why He chooses whom. Any biblical proof that some have been snatched from obscurity and exalted to prosperity without losing their integrity? Any examples of prosperous people who kept their balance while walking on the wire? Sure, several of them.

● Daniel was lifted from a lowly peon in a boot camp at Babylon to a national commander in charge of one-third of the kingdom (Daniel 6:1–2).

74

- Amos was promoted from a fig-picker in Tekoa, nothing more than an ancient sharecropper, to the prophet of God at Bethel, the royal residence of the king (Amos 7:14–15).
- Job was a rancher in Uz when God prospered him and granted him financial independence (Job 1:1–5).

And not one of the three lost his integrity in the process.

But the classic example is David, according to the last three verses of Psalm 78:

> He also chose David His servant, and took him from the sheepfolds; from the care of the ewes with suckling lambs He brought him, to shepherd Jacob His people, and Israel His inheritance. So he shepherded them according to the integrity of his heart, and guided them with his skillful hands.

As Jehovah scanned the Judean landscape in search of Saul's successor, He found a youth in his mid-teens who possessed a unique combination:

> the humility of a servant,
>> the heart of a shepherd,
>>> the hands of skill.

And by his thirtieth birthday, Jesse's youngest held the premier office in his nation. King. At his fingertips was a vast treasury, unlimited privileges, and enormous power.

And how did he handle such prosperity? Read that final verse again. He shepherded the nation ''according to integrity.'' He was Carlyle's ''one in a hundred.''

Are *you*?

If so, when you give your word, you do it. Exactly as you said you would. Because integrity means you are verbally trustworthy. Furthermore, when the bills come due, you pay them. Because integrity means you are financially dependable. Also, when you're tempted to mess around with an illicit sexual affair, you resist. Because integrity means you are morally pure. You don't fudge because you're able to cover your tracks. Neither do you fake it because you're now a big shot. Being successful doesn't give anybody the right to call wrong right. Or the OK to say something's OK if it isn't OK.

Adversity or prosperity, both are tough tests on our balance. To stay balanced through adversity, resiliency is required. But to stay balanced through prosperity—ah, that demands *integrity*. The swift wind of compromise is a lot more devastating than the sudden jolt of misfortune.

That's why walking on a wire is harder than standing up in a storm. Height has a strange way of disturbing our balance.

Deepening Your Roots

Micah 6:8; Daniel 1:1–21; Proverbs 22:1

Branching Out

1. Quick—jot down the names of six people whom you deem successful. Put a word by each name that describes how that person handles his success. After you've done that, note your impressions or perhaps a lesson you can learn from your own evaluation.

2. Rate your success quotient—what's more important:
   - your level of success or your walk with God?
   - your staying successful or your keeping happy?
   - your retaining a position or your respect?

   Dialogue with a friend on how you answered these questions.

Unambitious Leadership

Let's take a look at the important balance between natural and spiritual leadership. A leader, obviously, must have some God-given natural qualities that cause others to respond to his or her *influence*. At the same time, the *Christian* leader must possess a marked degree of Spirit-directed, humble devotion to the Lord Jesus Christ . . . lest he fall into the category of a self-appointed, ambitious creature who simply loves the spotlight. It is upon this point I want to camp for a few minutes.

Dr. A. W. Tozer wrote:

A true and safe leader is likely to be one who has no desire to lead, but is forced into a position of leadership by the inward pressure of the Holy Spirit and the press of the external situation. Such were Moses and David and the Old Testament prophets. I think there was hardly a great leader from Paul to the present day but was drafted by the Holy Spirit for the task, and commissioned by the Lord of the Church to fill a position he had little heart for. I believe it might be accepted as a fairly reliable rule of thumb that the man who is ambitious to lead is disqualified as a leader.

Spiritual leaders, you see, are not made by majority

vote or ecclesiastical decisions, by conferences or synods. Only God can make them!

> For not from the east, nor from the west,
> Nor from the desert comes exaltation;
> But God is the Judge;
> He puts down one, and exalts another (Psalm 75:6–7).

This means, then, that God makes it *His* responsibility to prepare, nurture, train, and promote certain people to places of leadership. That's *His* business, not ours. Listen to Jeremiah 45:5:

> But you, are you seeking great things for yourself? Do not seek them. . . .

May those words never be forgotten. We live in a do-it-yourself era. We are programmed to think in terms of promotion, advertisement, public image, and appeal. Such things commercialize the ministry and smack of side-show tactics . . . or, to use Paul's words:

> ". . . walking in craftiness . . . adulterating the Word of God . . . preaching ourselves. . . . "

Do I address one who is gifted, capable, qualified to lead, but God has not yet promoted you? Let me warn you of the danger of *selfish ambition1*. Quietly and in subtle ways you can manipulate others to notice you, to be impressed with you. The cheap narcotic of ambition can deaden the pain of your inner conscience . . . but you can ride the crest of your self-made fame just so long. In the end, alas, it stings like a serpent.

Solomon's words fit well:

For the ways of a man are before the eyes of the LORD, And He watches all his paths. His own iniquities will capture the wicked, And he will be held with the cords of his sin (Proverbs 5:21–22).

Let me end on a positive note. God knows what He's about. If He has you sidelined, out of the action for awhile, He knows what He's doing. You just stay faithful . . . stay flexible . . . stay available . . . stay humble, like David with his sheep (even *after* he had been anointed king!). Learn your lessons well in the schoolroom of obscurity. God is preparing you as His chosen arrow. As yet your shaft is hidden in His quiver, in the shadows . . . but at the precise moment at which it will tell with the greatest effect, He will reach for you and launch you to that place of His appointment.

Deepening Your Roots
Joshua 1:1–5; Proverbs 25:6–7; Luke 14:1–11

Branching Out
1. Are you in a leadership position? Did you get there by your own efforts or do you sense God's intervention and appointing you to such a role? (Be honest!) I challenge you each morning to get down on your knees and seek God's power to keep you a loving, humble, and effective leader (or parent)—for *His* glory, not yours.
2. Not sure what you should be doing with your life? Do what David did: Stay put, work hard, take time for God, and leave your future with Him.

Pharisaism

Jesus opened a five-gallon can of worms the day He preached His sermon on the mount. There wasn't a Pharisee within gunshot range who wouldn't have given his last denarius to see Him strung up by sundown. Did they hate Him! They hated Him because He refused to let them get away with their phony religious drool and their super-spiritual ooze that was polluting the public.

The Messiah unsheathed His sharp sword of truth the day He ascended the mountain. When He came down that evening, it was dripping with the blood of hypocrites. If ever an individual exposed pride, Jesus did that day. His words bit into their hides like harpoons into whale blubber. Never in their notorious, smug careers had they been pierced with such deadly accuracy. Like bloated beasts of the deep they floated to the surface for all to see.

If there was one thing Jesus despised, it was the very thing every Pharisee majored in at seminary: showing off, or, to cushion it a bit, self-righteousness. They were the Holy Joes of Palestine, the first to enlist undiscerning recruits into the Royal Order of Back-Stabbers. They were past-masters in the practice of put-down prayers, and spent their days working on ways to impress others with their somber expression and monotonous, dismal drone. Worst of all, by sowing the seeds of legalistic thorns and nurturing them into forbidding vines of religious intolerance, the Pharisees prevented honest seekers from approaching their God.

Even today, the bite of legalism spreads a paralyzing venom into the Body of Christ. Its poison blinds our eyes, dulls our edge, and arouses pride in our hearts. Soon our love is eclipsed as it turns into a mental clipboard with a long checklist, a thick filter requiring others to measure up before we move in. The joy of friendship is fractured by a judgmental attitude and a critical look. It seems stupid to me that fellowship must be limited to the narrow ranks of predictable personalities clad in "acceptable" attire. The short haircut, clean-shaven, tailored suit look (with matching vest and tie, of course) seem essential in many circles. Just because I prefer a certain style or attire doesn't mean that it's best or that it's for everyone. Nor does it mean that the opposite is any *less* pleasing to God.

Our problem is a gross intolerance of those who don't fit *our* mold—an attitude which reveals itself in the stoic stare or a caustic comment. Such legalistic and prejudiced reactions will thin the ranks of the local church faster than fire in the basement or flu in the pew. If you question that, take a serious look at the Galatians letter. Paul's pen flowed with heated ink as he rebuked them for "deserting" Christ (1:6), "nullifying the grace of God" (2:21), becoming "bewitched" by legalism (3:1), and desiring "to be enslaved" by this crippling disease (4:9).

Sure . . . there are limits to our freedom. Grace *does not* condone license. Love has its biblical restrictions. The opposite of legalism is not "do as you please." But listen! The limitations are far broader than most of us realize. I can't believe, for example, that the only music God smiles on is highbrow or hymns. Why not country-folk or Dixieland as well? Nor do I believe the necessary garment for entering the Veil is a suit and tie. Why won't cutoffs or jeans and Hang Ten tee-shirts do just as well? Shocked? Let's remember who it is that becomes wrought-up over outward appearances. Certainly not God!

> . . . God sees not as man sees, for man looks at the outward appearance, but the LORD looks at the heart (1 Samuel 16:7b).

And who can prove that the only voice God will bless is the ordained minister on Sunday? How about the salesman Tuesday afternon or the high school teacher Friday morning?

It is helpful to remember that our Lord reserved His strongest and longest sermon not for struggling sinners, discouraged disciples, or even prosperous people, but for hypocrites, glory hogs, legalists—the present-day Pharisees.

The message on the mountain delivered that afternoon centuries ago echoes down the canyons of time with pristine force and clarity.

Listen to Matthew 6:1:

> Beware of practicing your righteousness before men to be noticed by them . . .

In other words, stop showing off! Stop looking down your nose at others who don't fill your pre-conceived mold. Stop displaying your own goodness. Stop calling attention to your righteousness. Stop lusting to be noticed. Implied in this is the warning to beware of those who refuse to stop such behavior. And then, to blaze that warning into their memories, He went on to give three specific examples of how people show off their own righteousness so that others might ooh and aah over them.

Matthew 6:2 talks about "when you give alms" or when you are involved in acts of charity assisting others in need. He says don't "sound a trumpet" when you do this. Keep it quiet . . . even a secret (6:4). Don't scream for attention like Tarzan swinging through the jungle. Stay out of the picture, remain anonymous. Don't expect to have your name plastered all over the place. Pharisees *love* to show off their gifts to others. They *love* to be made over, They *love* to remind others who did this and that, or gave such and such to so and so. Jesus says: Don't show off when you use your money to help somebody out.

Matthew 6:5 talks what to do "when you pray." He warns us against being supplicational showoffs who love to stand in prominent places and mouth meaningless mush in order to be seen and heard. Pharisees love syrupy words and sugar-crusted platitudes. They've got the technique for sounding high-and-holy down pat. Everything they say in their prayers causes listeners to think that this pious soul resides in heaven and was tutored at the feet of Michael the archangel and King James V. You're confident that they haven't had a dirty thought in the past eighteen years . . . but you're also quietly aware that there's a huge chasm between what is coming out of the showoff's mouth and where your head is right then. Jesus says, Don't show off when you talk with your Father.

Matthew 6:16 talks about what to do "when you fast." Now that's the time the showoff really hits his stride. He works overtime trying to appear humble and sad, hoping to look hungry and exhausted like some freak who just finished crossing the Sahara that afternoon. "Do not be as the hypocrites!" Christ commands. Instead, we ought to look and sound fresh, clean, and completely natural. Why? Because that's *real*—that's *genuine*—that's what He promises He will *reward*. Jesus says: Don't show off when you miss a couple or three meals.

Let's face it. Jesus spoke with jabbing, harsh words concerning the Pharisees. When it came to narrow legalism or self-righteous showing off, our Lord pulled no punches. He found it to be the only way to deal with those people who hung around the place of worship disdaining and despising other people. No less than seven times He pronounced "Woe to you"—because that's the only language a Pharisee understands, unfortunately.

Two final comments:

First . . . if you tend toward Pharisaism in any form, *stop it!* If you are the type of person who tries to bully others and look down at others (all the while thinking how impressed God must be to have you on His team) you are a twentieth century Pharisee. And frankly, that includes some who wear longer hair and prefer a guitar to a pipe organ. Pharisees can also delight in looking "cool."

Second . . . if a modern-day Pharisee tries to control your life, *stop him! Stop her!* Remind the religious phony that the splinter within your eye is between you and your Lord, and to pay attention to the tree trunk in his own eye. Chances are, however, that once an individual is infected, he will go right on nit-picking and self-praising for the rest of his shallow life, choked by the thorns of his own conceit. Pharisees, remember, are terribly hard of listening.

Deepening Your Roots
Proverbs 30:12; Matthew 7:1–5; 23:1–26

Branching Out
1. Pray with a child and speak his language. Learn from the child the wonder he has of life and the freedom and honesty with his words and thoughts. Try talking to God in that same way.
2. Go without a meal someday soon and use your lunch or dinner time to talk to and enjoy God. Don't tell anyone what you plan to do, or what you did.

Fear

We were rapidly descending through a night of thick fog at 200 miles per hour, but the seasoned pilot of the twin-engine Aero Commander was loving every dip, roll, and lurch. At one point he looked over at me, smiled, and exclaimed, "Hey, Chuck, isn't this great?" I didn't answer. As the lonely plane knifed through the overcast pre-dawn sky, I was reviewing every Bible verse I'd ever known and re-confessing every wrong I'd ever done. It was like hurtling 200 miles an hour down the Santa Ana Freeway with a white bedsheet wrapped across the windshield and your radio turned up just beneath the threshold of audible pain.

I couldn't believe my companion-in-flight. He was whistling and humming like it was all a bike ride through the park. His passenger, however, had ten fingernails imbedded in the cushion. I started longingly for something—*anything*—throught the blanket of white surrounding us. Our flight record may have indicated two passengers on the eerie Monday morning, but I can vouch for at least three. An unyielding creature called Fear and I shared the same seat.

Drifting in through cracks in the floorboards or filtering down like a chilling mist, the fog called Fear whispers omens of the unknown and the unseen. Surrounding individuals with its blinding, billowy robe, the creature hisses, "What if . . . what if . . . ?" One blast of its awful breath transforms saints into atheists, reversing a person's entire mind-set. Its bite releases a paralyzing venom in its victim, and it isn't long before doubt begins to dull the vision. To one who falls prey to this attack, the creature displays no mercy. As we fall, it steps on our face with the weight of a Sherman tank . . . and laughs at our crippled condition as it prepares for another assault.

Fear. Ever met this beast? Sure you have. It creeps into your cockpit by a dozen different doors. Fear of failure. Fear of heights. Fear of crowds. Fear of disease. Fear of rejection. Fear of unemployment. Fear of what others are saying about you. Fear of moving away. Fear of height or depth or distance or death. Fear of being yourself. Fear of buying. Fear of selling. Fear of financial reversal. Fear of war. Fear of the dark. Fear of being alone.

Lurking in the shadows around every imaginable corner, it threatens to poison your inner peace and outward poise. Bully that it is, the creature relies on scare tactics and surprise attacks. It watches for your vulnerable moment, then picks the lock that safeguards your security. Once inside, it strikes quickly to transform spiritual muscle into mental mush. The prognosis for recovery is neither bright nor cheery.

David's twenty-seventh psalm, however, is known to contain an unusual effective antitoxin. With broad, bold strokes, the monarch of Israel pens a prescription guaranteed to infuse iron into our bones. He meets Fear face-to-face at the door of his dwelling with two questions:

> Whom shall I dread?
> Whom shall I fear?

He slams the door in Fear's face with the declaration:

> My heart will not fear . . . in spite of this I shall be confident (v. 3).

He then whistles and hums to himself as he walks back into the family room, kitchen, office, or bedroom, reminding himself of the daily dosage required to counteract Fear's repeated attacks:

> PRAYER: I have asked from the LORD (v. 4).
> VISION: I behold the beauty of the LORD (v. 4).
> GOD'S WORD: I meditate in His temple (v. 4).
> GOD'S PROTECTION: In the day of trouble He will conceal me/hide me/lift me (v. 5).
> MOMENT-BY-MOMENT WORSHIP: I will sing (v. 6).
> REST: I had believed . . . wait for the Lord (vv. 13–14).
> DETERMINATION: Let your heart take courage (v. 14).

Oh, how I needed this prescription in that dark cockpit as we dropped thousands of feet through the fog. Could it be that a cold overcast obscures your horizons right now? Tell you what—let's share the same seat and relax for a change. God's never missed the runway through all the centuries of fearful fog. But you might fasten your seat belt, friend. It could get a little rough before we land.

Deepening Your Roots
Psalm 27; 2 Timothy 1:7; Isaiah 51:12–16

Branching Out
1. State three fears you have. Choose one and read some other material that could help reduce some of that fear. And slam the door in Fear's face by claiming God's protection as David did.
2. Take another of your fears from the above list. Decide what would be the worst that could happen if the fear were real? How is God bigger than the fear?

Courage

Miss Hurricane Carla was a flirt.

She winked at Galveston, whistled at Palacios, waved at Corpus Christi, waltzed with Port Lavaca, and walked away with Rockport, Aransas Pass, and half of Matagorda Island. Her previous escort warned us that she was a wicked woman . . . but few fishermen believed those rumors that blew in from the fickle waters of the gulf. Not only was she wicked, she was expensive and *mean*. That mid-September date fifteen years ago cost us 400 million dollars . . . and forty lives.

One of my closest friends lived through that ordeal. He spent two terrible days and sleepless nights in his attic, surrounded by rattlesnakes, water moccasins, and other sassy visitors who had been flushed out of their habitat. Does he have the stories to tell! I would compare his courage—and the courage of hundreds like him who endured the dangers of Carla's rage—to anyone who has courted one of death's sisters and lived to describe the romance.

COURAGE. It has several names: bravery, valor, fearlessness, audacity, chivalry, heroism, confidence, nerve . . . and a few *nicknames:* guts, grit, gristle, backbone, pluck, spunk. But whatever the name, it's never met its match. The heights of the Himalayas only encourage it. The depths of the Caribbean merely excite it. The sounds of war stimulate it. The difficulty of a job motivates it. The demands of competition inspire it. Criticism challenges it . . . adventure arouses it . . . danger incites it . . . threats quicken it.

COURAGE. That's another word for inner strength, presence of mind against odds, determination to hang in there, to venture, persevere, withstand hardship. It's got *keeping* power. It's what kept the pioneers rolling forward in those covered wagons in spite of the elements and mountains and flaming arrows. It's what makes the amputee reject pity and continue to take life by the throat. It's what forces every married couple having trouble *never* to say, "Let's terminate." It's what encourages the divorcee to face tomorrow. It's what keeps the young mother with the kids in spite of a personal energy crisis. It's what keeps a nation free in spite of attacks. As Thomas Jefferson wrote in his letter to William Stevens Smith:

> The tree of liberty must be refreshed from time to time with the blood of patriots and tyrants. It is its natural manure.

COURAGE. David had it when he grabbed his sling in the Valley of Elah. Daniel demonstrated it when he refused to worship Nebuchadnezzar's statue in Babylon. Elijah evidenced it when he faced the prophets of Baal on Carmel. Job showed it when he was covered with boils and surrounded by misunderstanding. Moses used it when he stood against Pharaoh and refused to be intimidated. The fact is, *it's impossible to live victoriously for Christ without courage*. That's why God's thrice spoken command to Joshua is as timeless as it is true:

Be strong and courageous! (Joshua 1:6, 7, 9).

Are you? Honestly now—are you? Or are you quick to quit . . . ready to run when the heat rises?

Let it be remembered that real courage is not limited to the battlefield or the Indianapolis 500 or bravely catching a thief in your house. The *real* tests of courage are much broader . . . much deeper . . . much quieter. They are the *inner* tests, like remaining faithful when nobody's looking . . . like enduring pain when the room is empty . . . like standing along when you're misunderstood.

You will never be asked to share your attic with a rattler. But every day, in some way, your courage will be tested. Your tests may not be as exciting as a beachhead landing or sailing around Cape Horn or a space walk. It may be as simple as saying no, as uneventful as facing a pile of dirty laundry, or as unknown as a struggle within yourself between right and wrong. God's medal of honor winners are made in secret because their most courageous acts occur down deep inside . . . away from the hurricane of public opinion . . . up in the attic, hidden from public knowledge.

Deepening Your Roots
Daniel 3; Hebrews 13:6; Proverbs 29:25

Branching Out
1. We've all been brave at some point in time—whether we were recognized for it or not. What's a courageous act you've done?
2. What's something you can be courageous about today?

Songless Saints

I was on a scriptural safari. Prowling through the Ephesian letter, I was tracking an elusive, totally unrelated verse when God's sharp sword flashed, suddenly slicing me to the core.

> . . . speaking to one another in psalms and hymns and spiritual songs, singing and making melody with your heart to the Lord (Ephesians 5:19).

Everyone knows Ephesians 5:18, where we are told to "be filled with the Spirit" . . . but have you ever noticed that verse 18 ends with a comma, not a period? The next verse described the very first result of being under the Spirit's control . . . *we sing!* We make melody with our hearts. We communicate His presence within us by presenting our own, individual concert of sacred music to Him.

Let's take it another step. The church building is not once referred to in Ephesians 5. I mention that because we Christians have so centralized our singing that we seldom engage in it once we drive away from the building with stained glass and an organ. Stop and think. Did you sing on the way *home* from church last Sunday? How about Monday, when you drove to work . . . or around the supper table . . . or Tuesday as you dressed for the day? Chances are, you didn't even sing before or after you spent some time with the Lord *any* day last week.

Why? The Spirit-filled saint is a song-filled saint! Animals cn't sing. Neither can pews or pulpits or Bibles or buildings. Only you. And your melody is broadcast right into heaven—live—where God's antenna is always receptive . . . where the soothing strains of your song are always appreciated.

Believe me, if Martin Luther lived today, he'd be heartsick. That rugged warrior of the faith had two basic objectives when he fired the reformation cannon into the sixteenth century wall of spiritual ignorance. First, he wanted to give the people a Bible they could read on their own, and second, to give them a hymnal so they could sing on their own. The Bible we have, and its words we read. The hymnal we have, but where, oh, where has the melody gone? Mr. Songless Saint is about as acquainted with his hymnal as his six year old daughter is with the Dow Jones averages. Christians know more verses by heart from Ecclesiastes and Ezekiel than from the well-worn hymnal they use over 100 times a year! We simply do not sing as often as we ought, and therein lies the blame and the shame.

Allow me to offer a few corrective suggestions:

Whenever and wherever you sing, concentrate on the words. If it helps, close your eyes. Let yourself get so lost in the accompanying melody that you momentarily forget where you are and what others might think.

Frankly, I find it impossible to praise my Lord in song at the same time I feel self-conscious.

Make a concentrated effort to add one or two songs to your day. Remind yourself periodically of the words of a chorus or hymn you love and add them to yor driving schedule or soap-and-shower time.

Sing often with a friend or members of your family. It helps melt down all sorts of invisible barriers. Singing before grace at mealtime in the evening is *so* enjoyable, but I warn you, you may become addicted.

Blow the dust off your record player and put on some beautiful music in the house. The family atmosphere will change for the better if you do this occasionally. And don't forget to sing along, adding your own harmony and ''special effects.''

Never mind how beautiful or pitiful you may sound. Sing loud enough to drown out those defeating thoughts that normally clamor for attention. Release yourself from that cage of introspective reluctance—**SING OUT!** You are not auditioning for the choir, you're making melody with your heart.

If you listen closely when you're through, you may hear the hosts of heaven shouting for joy. Then again, it might be your neighbor . . . screaming for relief.

Deepening Your Roots

1 Chronicles 16:7–36; Psalm 30:9; 100:2; 149:1–5; Luke 19:40

Branching Out

1. Sing a song in place of saying grace today.
2. Turn on the stereo, choose a record, play it . . . and sing along with the music.
3. Take a walk or drive by yourself, and as you go create your own music and song for God. He'll love it.

Back to the Basics

The late football strategist, Vince Lombardi, was a fanatic about fundamentals. Those who played under his leadership often spoke of his intensity, his drive, his endless enthusiasm for the guts of the game. Time and again he would come back to the basic techniques of blocking and tackling. On one occasion his team, the Green Bay Packers, lost to an inferior squad. It was bad enough to lose . . . but to lose to *that* team was absolutely inexcusable. Coach Lombardi called a practice the very next morning. The men sat silently, looking more like whipped puppies than a team of champions. They had no idea what to expect from the man they feared the most.

Gritting his teeth and staring holes through one athlete after another, Lombardi began:

"Ok, we go back to the basics this morning. . . . "

Holding a football high enough for all to see, he continued to yell:

". . . gentlemen, *this* is a *football!*"

How basic can you get? He's got guys sitting there who have been playing on gridirons for fifteen to twenty years . . . who know offensive and defensive plays better than they know their kids' names . . . and he introduces them to a football! That's like saying, "Maestro, this is a baton." Or, "Librarian, this is a book." Or, "Marine, this is a rifle." Or, "Mother, this is a skillet." Talk about the obvious!

Why in the world would a seasoned coach talk to professional athletes like that? Apparently it worked, for no one else ever led his team to three consecutive world championships. But—*how?* Lombardi operated on a simple philosophy. He believed that excellence could be best achieved by perfecting the basics of the sport. Razzle-dazzle, crowd-pleasing, risk-taking plays would fill a stadium (for a while) and even win some games (occasionally), but in the final analysis the consistent winners would be the teams that played smart, heads-up, hard-nose football. His strategy? Know your position. Learn how to do it right. Then do it with all your might! That simple plan put Green Bay, Wisconsin, on the map. Before Lombardi's advent, it was a frozen whistle stop between Oshkosh and Iceland.

What works in the game of football works in the church as well. But in the ranks of Christendom, it's easy to get a little confused. Change that: a *lot* confused. When you say "church" today, it's like ordering a malt . . . you've got thirty-one flavors to choose from. You can select wheeler-dealers, snake handlers, positive thinkers, or self realizers. Rock bands with colored lights, hooded "priests" with bloody knives, shaved heads with pretty flowers, and screaming showmen with healing lines are also available. It that doesn't satisfy, search for your favorite "ism" and it's sure to turn up: humanism, liberalism, extreme Calvinism, political activism, anticommunism, supernatural spiritism, or fighting fundamentalism.

But wait! What are the absolute basics of "the church"? What is the foundational task of a biblically oriented local assembly? Filtering out everything that isn't essential, what's left? Let's listen to the Coach. He tells us we have *four* major priorities if we're going to call ourselves a church:

> teaching . . . fellowship . . . breaking bread . . . prayer (Acts 2:42).

To these four we are to "continually devote ourselves." Solid, balanced, "winning" churches keep at the task of perfecting those basics. These form the *what* aspect of the church.

The *how* is equally important. Again, the Coach addresses the team. He declares that the church getting the job done is engaged in:

> . . . equipping the saints for the work of service, to the building up of the body . . . (Ephesians 4:12).

"Hey, that's easy," you say. "How simple can you get?" you ask. Are you ready for a shocker? The toughest job you can imagine is maintaining these basic assignments. Most people have no idea how easy it would be to leave the essentials and get involved in other activities.

Believe me—there is a steady stream of requests from good, wholesome, helpful sources to use the pulpit as a platform for their cause. I repeat—good and whole-some things, but not essential . . . not directly related to our basic purpose: the interpretation, the exposition, the application of Holy Scripture . . . with relevance, enthusiasm, clarity, and conviction. First and foremost, that is what a pulpit ministry is all about.

But churches like that are so rare across our land, it makes you want to stand up and say:

"Ladies and gentlemen, *this* is a *Bible!*"

Deepening Your Roots
Acts 2:42–47; Ephesians 4:12–16; Ephesians 2:19–22

Branching Out
1. While you're in church this Sunday make sure you do the four basics: take in some teaching; talk to at least three other people; participate in communion; and pray.
2. Make arrangements to have lunch after church next week with a friend. Include in your dinner talk two positive or important truths you learned from the message or gained by being among other Christians.

Busyness

Run, saint, run!

Appointments, activities, assignments . . . run!

Demands, decisions, deadlines . . . run!

Schedules, services, seminars . . . run!

Plans, programs, people . . .

Stop!

Step aside and sit down. Let your motor idle down for a minute and think for a change. Think about your pace . . . your busyness. How did you get trapped in that squirrel cage? What is it down inside your boiler room that keeps pouring the coal on your fire? Caught your breath yet? Take a glance back over your shoulder, say, three or four months. Could you list anything significant accomplished? How about feelings of fulfillment—very many? Probably not, if you're honest.

There's a man in Oklahoma City named James Sullivan who knows how you feel. Back in the 1960s he blew his town wide open developing the largest Young Life Club in the nation. And that's not all he blew wide open. Along the way, he managed to sacrifice his health and his family. Blazing along the success track, Sullivan became a difficult man to keep up with, let alone live with. His wife, Carolyn, was getting tired. So were his children, who seldom saw their father. When they did, he was irritable. Although he never realized it at the time, Sullivan's full-throttle lifestyle was actually an escape technique. Listen to his admission in his book, *The Frog Who Never Became a Prince*:

> I was a man who existed in a shell . . . guilt, resentment, and hatred welled up within me. The resulting hard feelings I developed became almost insurmountable.

What happened? Wasn't this guy a Christian, working for Jesus, spreading the Gospel, reaching the youth? Yes, indeed. But Sullivan substituted activity for living, busyness for meaningful priorities. One Thanksgiving Carolyn asked him a question as he was racing out the door to speak at some camp. "Do you know, or do you even care, that from the middle of September until today, you have not been home *one* night?" Not long after that, she broke emotionally. He contemplated suicide.

STINGING WORDS—BUT TRUE. SOUND FAMILIAR? HERE'S WHY:

Busyness rapes relationships. It substitutes shallow frenzy for deep friendship. It promises satisfying dreams but delivers hollow nightmares. It feeds the ego but starves the inner man. It fills a calendar but fractures a family. It cultivates a program but plows under priorities.

Many a church boasts about its active program: "Something every night of the week for everybody." What a shame! With good intentions the local assembly can *create* the very atmosphere it was designed to curb. The One who instructed us to "be still and know that I am God" must hurt when He witnesses our frantic, compulsive, agitated motions. In place of a quiet, responsive spirit we offer Him an inner washing machine—churning with anxiety, clogged with too much activity, and spilling over with resentment and impatience. Sometimes He must watch our convulsions with a heavy sigh.

My mentor was wise. He once declared:

> Much of our activity these days is nothing more than a cheap anesthetic to deaden the pain of an empty life.

SEARCHING WORDS—BUT TRUE. WANT TO CHANGE? HERE'S HOW:

First, *admit it*. You are too busy. Say it to yourself . . . your family . . . your friends. Openly and willingly *acknowlege* that what you are doing is wrong and something must be done—now. I did that recently and, through tears, my family and I cleared some bridges the thorns of neglect had overgrown.

Second, *stop it*. Starting today, refuse every possible activity which isn't absolutely necessary. Sound ruthless? So is the clock. So is your health. Start saying no. Practice saying it aloud a few times—form the letters in your mouth. The phonetic structure of this two-letter word really isn't all that difficult. If feasible, resign from a committee or two . . . or three or four. Quit feeling so important. They'll get somebody else. Or maybe they'll wise up and adopt a better plan.

Third, *maintain it*. It's easy to start fast and fade

quickly. Discuss with your family some ways of investing time with *them*—without the TV . . . without apologies for playing and laughing and doing nutty, fun things . . . without gobs of money having to be spent to "entertain" you.

Fourth, *share it*. It won't be very long before you begin gleaning the benefits of putting first things first. Tell others. Infect them with some germs of your excitement. Believe me, there are a lot of activity-addicts within the fellowship of faith who'd love to stop running . . . if they only knew how.

Ask James Sullivan. His nickname is "Frog." By the time he got kissed, it was almost too late.

Almost.

Deepening Your Roots
Psalm 127; Ecclesiastes 2:22–26; Matthew 6:25–34

Branching Out
1. Talk to a friend or your family (spouse *and* children) and ask them this question: Am I too busy, rushing about, involved in too many activities? If they say "yeah," then talk further on what you should eliminate from your life. Then do it!
2. Go back to a friend you've offended by never writing, visiting with, etc. Apologize and let him know you're trying to give people more of a priority in life than projects or activities.

Spiritual Leadership

Leadership is *influence*. To the extent we influence others, we lead them. Lord Montgomery implied this when he wrote . . .

> Leadership is the capacity and will to rally men and women to a common purpose, and the character which inspires confidence.

We could name many great people who did just that, whether they were military personnel, athletic coaches, political figures, business executives, salesmen, or spiritual statesmen. *Influence* best describes the effect of their lives.

If I were asked to name some of the standard qualities or characteristics usually found among natural-born leaders, I would list:

Enthusiasm	Inquisitiveness	Flexibility
Optimism	Independence	Sense of humor
Persistence	Friendliness	Discipline
Ambition	Adventurousness	Creativity
Competitiveness	Security	Practicality
Knowledge	Decisiveness	Aggressiveness
Insight	Integrity	Poise

None can deny that these are standard qualities found in "natural" leaders. But *my* question is: Are these qualities necessary in "spiritual" leaders, too? Before you answer too quickly, I would refer you to some biblical leaders who would've done rather poorly on a "natural" leadership test. The incredible thing is that God picked people whom we would have overlooked!

How about withdrawn, insecure, fearful, doubting Moses? (Read Exodus 3:10–4:14.) Or the uncultured, negative, ill-prepared, unwanted, dogmatic, clumsy fig-picker Amos? (Get acquainted with him in Amos 7:10–17.) And we dare not forget impulsive, short-sighted, boastful Peter, who frequently suffered from foot-in-mouth disease!

I am not suggesting these men did not have any natural traits of leadership—but rather that they broke the mold of what we generally classify as "a model leader." God's remnant of leaders is often a ragged lot . . . frequently made up of fresh-thinking, non-conforming, even weird-looking characters who desperately love the Lord Jesus Christ and are remarkably available to Him and His will. These people (and you may be one!) possess the basic ingredients of faith, vision, teachability, determination, and love—and they are involved in changing the world.

When I read that God is searching this planet for men and women (please stop and read 2 Chronicles 16:9a and Ezekiel 22:30), I do not find that He has a structured, well-defined frame into which they must fit. In fact, some of those God used most effectively were made up of the strangest mixture you could imagine. If you doubt this, check out that rough gang of 400 indebted unorganized malcontents that surrounded David in the *cave of Adullam* (1 Samuel 22:1–2). I find myself extraordinarily challenged to trace these men through the balance of David's life, and discover that these became his elite, courageous band of fighting men—heroes, if you please—from whom a number of leaders emerged.

I believe you anticipate my point. Let's be as open and flexible and tolerant as God is! Perhaps *you* don't fit the mold. Maybe you don't embrace the party-line system, so you're beginning to think "I'm not useful to God—I'll never be a leader in the ranks of Christianity." Take heart, discouraged believer! I rather suspect that others of you are about to write off your maverick *kids*. Listen, they may be right on target. God may have a distinct, unique role of leadership just for that youngster of yours. Hang in there, parents! These young people may look and sound strange to some adults . . . but I'm not about to sigh and ask why. For all we know, God is on the verge of doing something great through their leadership.

Let me assure you—if all the adults had written off a young, repulsive, aggressive, strong-willed teenager thirty years ago . . . the book you hold in your hands would have never existed.

Deepening Your Roots
Exodus 3:10–4:14; Amos 7:10–17; 2 Chronicles 16:9a; Ezekiel 22:30

Branching Out
1. Name someone you know who is in a leadership position. Now, name a weakness they have as a leader. Pray for that person and ask that God would be strong where he is weak.
2. Are you a leader? If so, ask God how you could improve in your leadership skills. (Note an area you think God is zeroing in on.)
3. Afraid of leadership? Feel totally inadequate to lead? That's OK. But check your heart and make sure you are open and willing to allow God to use you as a leader if that's His pleasure. Remember Moses!

A Fire for Cold Hearts

It happened in a large, seventy-five-year-old stone house on the west side of Houston. A massive stairway led up to several bedrooms. The den down below was done in rough-hewn boards with soft leather chairs and a couple of matching sofas. The wet bar had been converted into a small library, including a shelf of tape recordings and a multiple-speaker sound system. The ideal place to spend a weekend . . . unfortunately, my wife and I were there just for the evening.

The smell of char-broiled T-bones drifted through the rooms. The ladies laughed in the kitchen as they fussed around with ranch-style baked beans, a variety of salads, and homemade pies. Everybody knew everybody. An easy, relaxing atmosphere made you want to kick off your shoes and run your fingers over the thick, black hair of the sleeping Labrador retriever sprawled across the hearth of a crackling fireplace.

The host, a lifelong Christian friend, leaned his broad shoulders against the mantel as he told of the bass that got away last week. While the guys chided him loudly for exaggerating ("it had to weigh ten to twelve pounds!"), my eyes ran a horizontal path across the carved message on the mantel. The room was too dark to read what it said from where I sat. I was intrigued and strangely drawn from my overstuffed chair to get a closer look.

I ran my fingers along the outline of each letter as my lips silently formed the words:

IF YOUR HEART IS COLD
    MY FIRE CANNOT WARM IT.

"Hmmmm," I thought, "how true."

Fireplaces don't warm hearts. Neither does fine furniture nor a four-car garage nor a full stomach nor a job with a six-figure salary. No, a cold heart can be warmed only by the fire of the living God.

I settled back down, stayed quiet, and mused over those thoughts. I even prayed as I stared into the fire:

"Lord, keep my heart warm. Stop me when I rev my motor and get to moving too fast toward stuff I think will make me happy. Guard me from this stupid tendency to substitute things for You."

The dinner bell broke the spell. I stood up with all the men and we strolled toward the patio. I took a quick glance to remind myself of the words on the mantel one more time. The logs were now burned down to embers, and in the glow I remembered:

IF YOUR HEART IS COLD
    MY FIRE CANNOT WARM IT.

I thanked God for His fire that has never burned down.

That memorable scenario happened over twenty years ago. My heart has, since then, occasionally cooled off.

Today, however, it is warm because He never left me when I was cold.

Deepening Your Roots
Deuteronomy 8:11–14; Matthew 24:12; Revelation 2:4–5

Branching Out
1. How would you rate the temperature of your heart?

hot; excited about God	semi-warm
burning zeal	lukewarm
very warm	cold
warm	icy

2. Ask God to rekindle the flame by bringing you a friend to pray with daily.
3. Build a fire tonight, roast marshmallows or pop corn in the fireplace, and talk with whoever is present (maybe just God) about the need to always stay close to Him. If you don't have a fireplace, visit a friend's house who has one, or drop in on a restaurant you know that keeps the wood burning.

Biblical Illiteracy

Standing ankle deep in snow, I copied the following inscription from the main wall near the old iron gate that leads to the campus of Harvard University:

> After God had carried us safe to New England and we had builded our houses, provided necessaries for our livelihood, reared convenient places for God's worship and settled the civil government, one of the next things we longed for and looked after was to advance learning and perpetuate it to posterity, dreading to leave an illiterate ministry to the churches when our present ministers lie in the dust.

No, you didn't make a mistake in your reading. The oldest institution of higher learning in our nation, founded just sixteen years after the Pilgrims landed at Plymouth, was established for the stated purpose of perpetuating an educated, well-trained body of godly men who would proclaim God's Word with intelligence, conviction, and authority. This was carried out until European liberalism, conviction, and authority. This was carried out until European liberalism, with its subtle narcotic of humanism and socialism, paralyzed the nerve centers of theological thought in our great land. Putting it bluntly, when the storm troopers of that damnable heresy captured the flag of biblical Christianity, all the forces of hell broke loose! It is safe to say that since that time, Mr. and Mrs. American Christian have been gasping for fresh, clean air beneath the suffocating blanket of sterile religion, Bible-less preaching, and lukewarm formalities like Laodicea of old. Except for a few, isolated islands of virility and hope, the tide has risen sharply and swept away the landmarks of genuine, Century One Christianity.

But all is not lost, believe me. We have the challenge and opportunity of standing erect against the tide of biblical illiteracy. We can face the flood without fear . . . *if* we continue to grow in grace and knowledge of our Lord and Savior (2 Peter 3:18). God has promised that we shall be blessed and protected *if* we will equip ourselves for the battle. But wait. . . . Look back at those "ifs." . . . If we grow . . . if we equip ourselves. *Are you?* Peel off that old mask and stare at yourself. Are YOU REALLY GROWING, spiritually? Are your spiritual muscles getting developed—I mean *really* getting developed? Are you drinking at the well of living water *daily* . . . or at least on a regular basis, *on your own?* Is your faith claiming specific objectives . . . or just collecting dust? How are your quiet times with the Lord—are they meaningful or miserable, are they fresh or forced?

How about my suggesting a biblical project for the next few months before you settle down for a long winter's nap? Pick one of the following for yourself and refuse to quit until it's completed . . . or create one of your own.

- Read the entire book of James aloud each week from now until New Years Day. (Or choose your own—preferably a short one.)
- Make a list of the arguments you hear from others most often *against* becoming a Christian. Then search the Scriptures for specific passages that give you insight and answers. (Read 1 Peter 3:14–15 first.)
- Commit to memory an entire chapter of one of your favorite Bible books . . . like Matthew 6 or John 15 or Romans 8 (or 12) or 1 Corinthians 13 or James 3 or 1 John 1. Do this by the end of the year.
- Find a biblical passage on prayer. Go to it every day with at least six of your most crucial needs. Leave room on the right side of your list to record the time and way God answered your requests. Do not stop until you are confident you should.

I cannot guarantee instant growth . . . nor can I promise that this will be easy. But after all, good soldiers of the cross have victory in mind, not luxury (please read 2 Timothy 2:1–4). And if I read my American history book correctly, I don't recall much being accomplished, spiritually or otherwise, without sacrifice and hardship. Resisting the tide is always hard work.

Brace up, island-dweller. When the battle's done and the victory's won, we will have plenty of time to take it easy and soak up the Son—an eternity, in fact.

Deepening Your Roots

2 Timothy 2:1–4; 1 Peter 2:2–3; Revelation 3:15, 16

Branching Out

1. Do two of the assignments in the article.
2. Visit a Christian bookstore and purchase a book that addresses an issue you're struggling with or need to be informed about. Read it!

Taking God Seriously

Comic caveman "B.C." leans on one of the strip's ever-present boulders. The rock is inscribed "Trivia Test," and B.C. is administering the exam to one of his deadpan prehistoric buddies.

"Here's one from the Bible," he says. "What were the last words uttered by Lot's wife?"

Without a moment's hesitation his skin-clad friend replies: "*The heck with your fanatical beliefs, I'm going to take one last look!*"

She may not have said it, but that's what she was thinking—*or worse*.

The sordid account of Sodomite lifestyle is graphically portrayed in Genesis 19. And it's anything but funny. The place was shot through with open and shameless perversions. According to verse 4, these were practiced by

> . . . both young and old, all the people from every quarter.

The vile city of Sodom would've made New York's sleazy Forty-second Street look like a bike ride along old Cape Cod. It was gross. Absolutely and completely degenerate. Over-populated with disgustingly wicked weirdos—professionals in the world of porno . . . the original nest of homos. Not pathetic sickies but willfully debased sinners who regularly practiced indecent and degrading acts on one another. In God's evaluation

> . . . their sin is exceedingly grave (Genesis 18:20b).

For some strange reason, Lot was drawn to Sodom. He and his family lived among these people and, no doubt, became accustomed to their ways, possibly viewing the pervasions as acceptable.

Then God stepped in. Jealous for Lot's deliverance, He clearly announced the evacuation plan:

> Escape for your life! Do not look behind you, and do not stay anywhere in the valley; escape to the mountains, lest you be swept away (Genesis 19:17).

What a gracious act! The Lord cared enough for Lot and his family to map out a plan that would lead to safety. Nothing complicated. No riddles. Just "run for your life—don't look back; don't stop until you're in the mountains."

Behind this serious warning, a severe extermination plot was unfolding. Doomsday was approaching. The worst holocaust in the history of ancient civilization.

> Then the LORD rained on Sodom and Gomorrah brimstone and fire from the LORD out of heaven, and He overthrew those cities and all the valley, and all the inhabitants of the cities, and what grew on the ground (Genesis 19:24–25).

I can almost feel the heat on my face as I read those words. The corrupt cities sank slowly as the waters of the Dead Sea bubbled over them and their charred inhabitants.

And Lot? Well, he was running for his life, with his two daughters nearby. The family was saved! No, not all the family. Mrs. Lot didn't make it. Apparently, she couldn't bring herself to believe God meant what He said.

It's interesting how Scripture records her demise:

> But his wife, from behind him, looked back; and she became a pillar of salt (Genesis 19:26).

QUESTION: Why was she "behind him"? Who knows for sure? I'd suggest she was still attached to that lifestyle. She willfully refused to cut off her emotional ties. All this business of running away and not looking back was awfully extreme, terribly unrealistic. To quote the caveman:

> *"The heck with your fanatical beliefs, I'm going to take one last look!"*

The bottom line of Mrs. Lot's philosophy could have been etched on her salt-block tombstone:

THERE'S NO NEED TO TAKE GOD SERIOUSLY.

I know of no philosophy more popular today. It's the reason we're caught these days in the do-your-own-thing *sin*drome. What a subtle web the spider of self has woven! Millions are stuck—and instead of screaming, "I'm caught!" they shout, with a smile, "I'm free!"

If you don't take God seriously, then there's no need

to take your marriage seriously . . . or the rearing of children . . . or such character traits as submission, faithfulness, sexual purity, humility, repentance, and honesty.

Take a long lick of salt this evening.

It stings, doesn't it?

Deepening Your Roots
Genesis 19:1–28; Jeremiah 6:13–19; Luke 17:20–33

Branching Out
1. Go to your kitchen, pull out the box of salt and sprinkle some in the palm of your hand. Now, take one long lick. Then come back and describe your reaction.
2. What are some things in your life that God has asked you to leave behind? Evaluate whether or not you've actually left these things behind, or if you keep "looking back." Purpose in your heart not to be like Mrs. Lot.

Nostalgia

Glen Campbell, with that guitar of his slung over his shoulder, has an uncanny ability to resurrect memories in the tender spots of my deepdown soul. His "Galveston" and "Gentle on My Mind" transport me to the dusty back roads of my memory as people and places step out of the shadows and visit with me for a brief moment or two. Crazy, isn't it? Almost weird! Suddenly, without announcement, nostalgia sweeps over me and I am trapped in its sticky web for an exhilarating experience that's always too brief to satisfy . . . too vivid to ignore . . . too deep to describe . . . too personal to share.

Nostalgia. That abnormal yearning within us to step into the time tunnel and recover the irrecoverable. That wistful dream, that sentimental journey taken within the mind—always traveled alone and therefore seldom discussed. Here's where it sometimes starts:

- A barefoot walk along a sandy beach.
- A quiet visit to the place you were raised.
- Listening to a rippling brook running alone over the rocks through a forest of autumn leaves.
- Singing the song of your *alma mater*.
- Looking over childhood photos in the family album.

- Watching your now-grown "child" leave home.
- Standing silently beside the grave of a close, personal friend or relative.
- The smell and sounds of a warm fireplace.
- An old letter, bruised with age, signed by one who loved you.
- Climbing to the top of a wind-swept hill.
- Getting alone—all alone—and reading aloud.
- Christmas Eve, late at night.
- Certain poems . . . certain melodies.
- Weddings . . . graduations . . . diplomas.
- Snow . . . sleds . . . toboggans.
- Saying goodbye.

Ah yes . . . you've been there. I can tell by that smile that you're trying to hide.

The holiday season brings it back with a special surge of poignancy. The smells from the kitchen, my loving wife, the laughter of the kids, the memories of home and family, the inexpressible gratitude to God for my home . . . my country . . . and my Savior . . . all converge upon me that one day as nostalgia's net tightens around me and holds me close within its imaginary ropes of security.

I have often wondered how Jesus must have entertained nostalgic feelings as He visited this planet He originally created. How moving is that passage which reads: *He came to His own . . .* (John 1:11). You see, when Jesus came as a man, He lived and walked among familiar territory. He was no stranger to this old earth . . . it was "to His own things" (literally) He returned—and my, how nostalgic the journey must have been for Him at times! Because He was not wanted, He

123

was driven to a life of silence, solitude, and simplicity. The mountains and the sea became His habitat. It was there he communed best with His Father, and it was there He trained His band of followers. Is it any wonder that the hills and the water still hold the mysteries of nostalgia and meditation?

Take a drive and get alone sometime this week—even if it's for only an hour. In the stillness of your surroundings, give nostalgia the go-ahead signal. Let it run free . . . release your grip and see where it takes you. That's one of my treasured pastimes during the holidays, and I want you to enjoy it with me.

If we meet together on the back roads of our memory, I will be so pleased—and I promise not to tell a soul. I'm good at keeping nostalgic secrets.

Deepening Your Roots
Matthew 26:6–13; Luke 22:7–19; 1 Thessalonians 3:6–13

Branching Out
1. Take a drive alone.
2. Recount a special holiday from your past and write someone else you shared it with why it brings back such fond memories. Pass on a bit of nostalgia.
3. Get the family album out of that box of ol' pictures hidden away and enjoy an evening of nostalgia.

Grace Revisited

Most of us did not learn to pray in church.

And we weren't taught it in school, or even in pajamas beside our bed at night. If the truth were known, we've done more praying around the kitchen table than anywhere else on earth. From our earliest years we've been programmed: If you don't pray, you don't eat. It started with Pablum in the high chair, and it continues through porterhouse at the restaurant. Right? Like passing the salt or doing the dishes, a meal is incomplete without it.

Our first impressions of communicating with the Almighty were formed in the high chair with cereal and pudding smeared all over our faces. We peeked and gurgled while everybody else sat silent and still. We than learned to fold our hands and close our eyes. Soon we picked up the cue to add our own "Amen" (which usually followed " . . . in Jesus' name"). Then came the day we soloed. We mumbled, looked around, got mixed up, then quickly closed with a relieved "Amen!" as we searched Mom and Dad's faces for approval.

Then we went through three very definite stages over the next eight to ten years of grace—stages that are common in most Christian families. Stage one . . . *snickering*. For some strange reason, prayer before the meal became the ''comedy hour'' when I was growing up. In spite of parental frowns and glares, threats and thrashings . . . my sister and I could *not* keep from laughing. I remember one time we giggled so long and so loud that our mother finally joined in. My older brother was praying (he usually remembered every missionary from Alaska to Zurich) and purposely refused to quit. He finished by praying for the *three of us*.

Stage two . . . *doubting*. This is a cynical cycle, a tough one to endure. We start questioning the habit—the custom. With an air of pseudo-sophistication, we think:

''What does it matter if I *don't* say grace?

''This is a ritual—it serves no purpose—God knows I'm grateful.''

Junior high years abound with these maverick thoughts. The whole scene of bowing heads and closing eyes and saying ''religious words'' suddenly seems childish . . . needless.

Stage three . . . *preaching*. This one is difficult to handle because it usually comes from well-meaning lips. Out of sincerity and a desire to prompt obedience, we use the time in prayer as an avenue to rebuke a family member or (very subtly) reinforce our own piety. Parents can easily fall into this manipulative technique, since it's impossible to be interrupted in prayer. The temptations of taking to the platform before our captive audience seem irresistible.

After passing through these stages, however, we begin to realize how good it is to cultivate this healthy habit. "Asking the blessing" is a sweet, much-needed, refreshing pause during hectic days. But since it occurs so often, the easiest trap to fall into is sameness. The perfunctory uttering of meaningless, repetitious clichés that become boring *even to God*. Our Lord Jesus thundered warning after warning against the empty verbosity which characterized the Pharisees.

Without claiming to have all the answers, I offer several suggestions a family can build on together.

1. *Think before you pray*. What's on the table? Call the food and drink by name. "Thank you, Lord, for the hot chicken-and-rice casserole in front of us. Thanks for the cold lemonade. . . . " What kind of day are you facing—or have you faced? Pray with those things in mind. Draw your prayer out of real life. Don't lapse into mechanical mutterings or convenient religious jargon. You're not just "saying a blessing," you're talking to your God!

2. *Involve others in prayer*. Try some sentence prayers around the table. Ask the family for requests.

3. *Sing your table blessing*. Try it a few times. After the family has recovered from the shock of shattering the norm, it might catch on. The Doxology, a familiar hymn, or a chorus of worship works great . . . and offers a change of pace. Holding hands can be meaningful.

4. *Keep it brief, please*. There's nothing like watching a thick film form over the gravy while you plow through all five stanzas of Wesley's "And Can It Be?" Remember what the blessing is all about—a pause to praise our faithful Provider—a moment of focus on the Giver of every good gift. You don't have to pray around the

world three times or highlight every relative between the poles and all the ships at sea. God's watching the heart, not totaling up the verbiage.

5. *Occasionally pray after the meal*. When the mood is loose or the meal is served in "shifts" or picnic-style settings, be flexible. An attitude of worship is occasionally much easier when the hunger pangs have eased up.

Is your prayer time at the table losing its punch? Here's a way to find out. When the meal is over and you get up to do the dishes, ask if anyone remembers what was prayed for. If they do, great. If they don't, sit back down at the table and ask why. You've got a lot more to be concerned about than a stack of dishes.

Deepening Your Roots
Psalm 104:10–15; 104:27–35; 107:1–9; Acts 27:35

Branching Out
1. Try one of the suggestions from today's reading.
2. Take a survey of ten people (or listen in on people praying at meal time) and inquire as to their prayers at mealtime. Are they always the same?

Thanksgiving

I've got a love affair going with Thanksgiving. It has been going on for over forty years, as far back as I can remember. Hands down, it's my favorite holiday of all.

Here's why.

First of all, it seems to blend together all we Americans hold precious and dear—without the sham and plastic mask of commercialism. Shopping centers jump from Halloween to Christmas. It's spooks to Santa . . . pumpkins to present . . . orange and black to red and green. It's doubtful that any of us has ever seen (or *will* ever see) a Pilgrim hype. Just can't be done. Except for grocery stores, merchants are mute when Thanksgiving rolls around.

Second, it highlights the home and family. Thanksgiving is synonymous with stuff that can be found only at home—the warmth of a fireplace, early morning fussing around in the kitchen, kids and grandkids, long distance phone calls, family reunions, singing around the piano, holding hands and praying before that special meal, the Cowboys versus somebody (they always beat) on the tube, a touch football game in the street or backyard, friends dropping by, pumpkin pie, homemade rolls, and six million calories.

It is a time of quiet reflection upon the past and an annual reminder that God has, again, been ever so faithful. The solid and simple things of life are brought into clear focus, so much so that everything else fades into insignificance.

Thanksgiving is good for our roots . . . it deepens them and strengthens them and thickens them . . . making our trunks and limbs more secure in spite of the threatening gale of our times. The meal, the memories, the music Thanksgiving brings have a way of blocking out the gaunt giant of selfishness and ushering in the sincere spirit of gratitude, love, and genuine joy.

Third, it drips with national nostalgia. For me, even more so than the Fourth of July. *That* holiday reminds us of a battle we won, giving us independence. This one takes us back to a simple slice of life over 350 years ago when our forefathers and foremothers realized their *de*pendence on each other to survive. With Thanksgiving comes a surge of renewed patriotism, a quiet inner peace that whispers, "*I am proud to be an American.*"

I recall, as a little barefoot boy with a cowlick of snow-white hair on my forehead, standing erect in my classroom and repeating the "Pledge of Allegiance" one Thanksgiving season. Our nation was at war and times were hard. My teacher had lost her husband on the bloodwashed shores of Normandy. As we later bowed our heads for prayer she wept aloud. I did too. All the class joined in. She stumbled through one of the most moving expressions of gratitude and praise that ever emerged from a soul plunged in pain. At that time in my young life, I fell strangely in love with Thanksgiving. Lost in sympathy and a boy's pity for his teacher, I walked home very slowly that afternoon. Although only a child, I had profound feelings of gratitude for my country . . . my friends . . . my school . . . my church . . . my family. I swore before God that I would fight to the end to keep this land free from foes who would want to take away America's distinctives and the joys of living in this good land. I have never forgotten my childhood promise. I never shall.

Thanksgiving puts steel into our patriotic veins. It reminds us of our great heritage. It carries us back with numbing nostalgia to that first dreadful winter at Plymouth where less than half the handful of people survived. It speaks in clear, crisp tones of forgotten terms, like: integrity . . . bravery . . . respect . . . faith . . . vigilance . . . dignity . . . honor . . . freedom . . . discipline . . . sacrifice . . . godliness. Its historic halls echo with the voices of Washington, Franklin, Jefferson, Adams, Henry, Lincoln, Lee, and Jackson who challenge us to trim off the fat of indolence, compromise, passivity, and the stigma of strife. It gives a depth of relevance and meaning to the nineteenth-century words of Katharine Lee Bates:

O beautiful for spacious skies,
    For amber waves of grain,
For purple mountain majesties
    Above the fruited plain!

O beautiful for patriot dream
    That sees beyond the years

Thine alabaster cities gleam
　　Undimmed by human tears!

—America! America!
God shed His grace on thee
And crown thy good with brotherhood
　　From sea to shining sea!

Nostalgia washes over me as I take a walk in the woods and reflect on those brave men and women whose bodies lie beneath white crosses—veterans who fought and died that I might live and be free—and as I consider those statesmen who hammered out our laws on the anvil of wisdom, compassion, and human dignity. People who cared about the future of this grand land, not just their own comforts. Visionaries. Tough-minded, clear-thinking, sacrificial souls who did more than talk about integrity. They modeled it.

Fourth and finally, it turns our heads upward. Just the word "Thanksgiving" prompts the spirit of humility. Genuine gratitude to God for His mercy, His abundance, His protection, His smile of favor. At this holiday, as at no other, we count our blessings and we run out of time before we exhaust the list. And best of all, life simplifies itself. At Thanksgiving we come back to the soil and the sun and the rain which combine their efforts to produce the miracle of life, resulting in food for our stomachs and shelter for our bodies . . . direct gifts from our God of grace. From the annals of our rich heritage, there has been preserved this announcement which was made 358 years ago. It says it all:

TO ALL YE PILGRIMS

Inasmuch as the great Father has given us this year an abundant harvest of Indian corn, wheat, beans, squashes, and garden vegetables, and has made the forests to abound with game and the sea with fish and clams, and inasmuch as He has protected us from the ravages of the savages, has spared us from pestilence and disease, has granted us freedom to worship God according to the dictates of our own conscience; now, I, your magistrate, do proclaim that all ye Pilgrims, with your wives and little ones, do gather at ye meeting house, on ye hill, between the hours of 9 and 12 in the day time, on Thursday, November ye 29th of the year of our Lord one thousand six hundred and twenty-three, and the third year since ye Pilgrims landed on ye Pilgrim Rock, there to listen to ye pastor, and render thanksgiving to ye Almighty God for all His blessings.

—William Bradford
Governor of Plymouth Colony, 1623

Deepening Your Roots
Exodus 12; Psalm 35:18; 66:1–9; 67

Branching Out
1. Say the pledge of allegiance some time during Thanksgiving Day or sing God Bless America or our national anthem.
2. Have each person (following the meal) state something about the person on their right for which they are thankful.

Gentleness

Tough and tender.

That's the combination every woman wants in a man. A balanced blend, an essential mixture of strong stability *plus* consideration, tact, understanding, and compassion. A better word is *gentleness* . . . but for some peculiar reason, that idea seems alien to the masculine temperament.

Observe the media-myth man. The man portrayed on the tube is rugged, hairy, built like a linebacker, drives a slick sports car, and walks with a swagger. In the beer ads he's all out for grabbing the gusto. With women he is a conqueror . . . fast and furious. In business he's "bullish." Even with a razor or hair dryer he's cocky, superconfident. If you don't believe it, *ask him*. The media-myth is, basically, *tough*. Spanish-speaking people would say he is known for his *machismo*. To the majority of young men—that's their hero, their masculine model.

Now let's understand something. A man *ought* to be a man! Few things are more repulsive than a man who carries himself like a woman . . . or wears stuff that suggests femininity. And we are living in an era when the roles are definitely eroding. I heard about a preacher who was conducting a wedding ceremony for a couple like this—both bride and groom having the same length hair and dressed in similar attire. Confused over their identity, he closed the ceremony with:

Would one of you kiss the bride?

The right kind of toughness—strength of character—ought to mark the man of today . . . but not only that. Tenderness—gentleness—is equally important.

God considers it so important He places it on the list of nine qualities He feels should mark the life of His children:

But the fruit of the Spirit is love, joy, peace, patience, kindness, goodness, faithfulness, gentleness, self-control; against such things there is no law (Galatians 5:22–23).

There it is . . . number eight. The Greek word translated "gentleness" is *prautes*, and it brims with meaning. In secular writings, the Greeks used it when referring to people or things that demonstrated a certain soothing quality—like an ointment that took the sting out of a burn. They also used this word to describe the right atmosphere which should prevail during a question-answer period in a classroom; the idea of discussing things without losing one's temper or becoming strongly defensive.

And think about this one. *Prautes* described the controlled conduct of one who had the power to act otherwise. Like a king who chose to be gracious instead of a tyrant. Like a military commander who patiently

135

trained an awkward squad of soldiers. Plato called *prautes* "the cement of society" as he used this word in the sense of politeness, courtesy, and kindness.

Gentleness has *three close traveling companions* in the New Testament:

1. It keeps company with agape-love (1 Corinthians 4:21).
2. It is a friend of meekness (2 Corinthians 10:1).
3. It is attached to humility (Ephesians 4:2).

Similarly, according to the New Testament, gentleness is the proper attitude when faced with *three difficult assignments*:

1. When faced with the need to exercise discipline in the Body of Christ (Galatians 6:1).
2. When faced with personal opposition (2 Timothy 2:25).
3. When faced with the truth of God's Word—being open and teachable (James 1:21).

Remember, our goal is balance . . . always balance. Not either-or, but both-and. Not just *tough*. That alone makes a man cold, distant, intolerant, unbearable. But tough *and* tender . . . gentle, thoughtful, teachable, considerate.

Both.

Like Christ.

Deepening Your Roots
Isaiah 40:11; 1 Corinthians 4:21; Ephesians 4:2; 1 Peter 3:8–12

Branching Out
1. What's a way you can show tenderness to another? Put your answer to work today. Be tender!
2. Exhibit gentleness in some way today by not losing your temper or becoming defensive.
3. Look for an incident today in which a person displayed a tender spirit. Compliment that person for his right attitude, words, or action.

One Long Extended Gift

Although it may be a little ahead of schedule, it's not too early to give some things away this Christmas. Not just on Christmas Day, but during the days leading up to December 25. We could call these daily gifts "our Christmas projects." Maybe one per day from now 'til then. Here are thirty-two suggestions. Take your choice.

- Mend a quarrel.
- Seek out a forgotten friend.
- Dismiss suspicion.
- Write a long overdue love note.
- Hug someone tightly and whisper, "I love you so."
- Forgive an enemy.
- Be gentle and patient with an angry person.
- Express appreciation.
- Gladden the heart of a child.
- Find the time to keep a promise.
- Make or bake something for someone else. Anonymously.
- Release a grudge.
- Listen.
- Speak kindly to a stranger.
- Enter into another's sorrow.
- Smile. Laugh a little. Laugh a little more.
- Take a walk with a friend.

138

- Kneel down and pat a dog.
- Read a poem or two to your mate or friend.
- Lessen your demands on others.
- Play some beautiful music during supper.
- Apologize if you were wrong.
- Talk together with the television off.
- Treat someone to an ice-cream cone.
- Do the dishes for the family.
- Pray for someone who helped you when you hurt.
- Fix breakfast for someone on Saturday morning.
- Give a soft answer even though you feel strongly.
- Encourage an older person.
- Point out one thing you appreciate most about someone you work with or live near.
- Offer to baby-sit for a weary mother.
- Give your teacher a break—be especially cooperative.

Let's make Christmas one long, extended gift of ourselves to others. Unselfishly. Without announcement. Or obligation. Or reservation. Or hypocrisy.

That *is* Christianity, isn't it?

Deepening Your Roots
Luke 21:1–4; Ephesians 2:8 and 9; Matthew 2:11

Branching Out
You come up with three assignments.

Year-end Reflections

Time to reflect. That would be my answer to the question: "What do you like most about the year-end holidays?"

Oh, the food is good—those delectable, fattening morsels that make Thanksgiving, Christmas, and New Year's so special. So are the parties and the people . . . the songs, the smiles, the smells. Each weaves its way into the fabric of our minds in such a beautiful manner that we live in the warmth of them for days. Sometimes *months*.

But the best those traditional holidays can offer, in my opinion, is time to reflect. To stand in front of the full-length mirror of memory and study the scene. Thoughtfully. Silently. Alone. At length. To trace the outline of the past without the rude interruption of routine tasks. To walk along the surf or stroll through a mountain pathway, taking time to stop and listen. And think. To sit by a crackling fireplace with all the lights out, staring into the heat, and letting thoughts emerge, drift, and linger. To turn over in the mind a line out of a poem. To hear some grand music played at sufficient volume that all petty noises and worries are submerged beneath the waves of stimulating sound.

Maybe it's part of what Charles Wesley meant by being "lost in wonder, love, and praise." A kind of solitary worship. An extended, unhurried leisure yielding rich benefits and deep insights. Invariably, those occasions leave me feeling grateful to God. Often I end up thanking Him specifically for something or someone that He provided in the yesterday of my life that makes my today much more meaningful.

It happened again last week. The day had been relaxing and fun. Night fell. One by one my family slipped into sleep. I put a couple more logs into the fireplace, slid into my favorite chair, and read for well over an hour. I came across a few thoughts put together by a long-time leader in the World Vision ministry—Ed Dayton. His words sent me back many, many years. Ed mentioned watching the short film called "The Giving Tree," a simple, fanciful piece about a tree who loved a boy.

They played hide 'n' seek in his younger years. He swung from her branches, climbed all over her, ate her apples, slept in her shade. Such happy, carefree days. The tree *loved* those years of the boy's childhood.

But the boy grew and spent less time with the tree. On one occasion the young man returned. "Come on, let's play," invited the tree . . . but the lad was only interested in money. "Take my apples and sell them," said the tree. He did . . . and the tree was happy.

He didn't return for a long time, but the tree smiled when he passed by one day. "Come, play, my friend. Come, play!" But the boy—now full grown—wanted to build a house for himself. "Cut off my branches and build your house," she offered. He did, and once again the tree was happy.

Years dragged by. The tree missed the boy. Suddenly, she saw him in the distance. "Come on, let's play!" But the man was older and tired of his world. He wanted to get away from it all. "Cut me down. Take my large trunk and make yourself a boat. Then you can sail away," said the tree. And that's exactly what he did . . . and the tree was happy.

Many seasons passed—summers and winters, windy days and lonely nights—and the tree waited. Finally, the old man returned . . . too old, too tired to play, to pursue riches, to build houses, or to sail the seas. "I have a pretty good stump left, my friend. Why don't you just sit down here and rest?" He did . . . and the tree was happy.[8]

I stared into the fire. I watched myself pass in review as I grew older with the tree and the boy. I identified with both—and it hurt.

How many Giving Trees have there been in my life? How many have released part of themselves so I might grow, accomplish my goals, find wholeness and satisfaction, and reach beyond the tiny, limited playground of my childhood? So, so many. Thank you, Lord, for each one. Their names could fill this page.

Now I, like the tree, have grown up. Now it's my turn to give. And some of that hurts. Apples, branches, sometimes the trunk. My rights, my will . . . and even my growing-up children.

So much to give. Thank you, Lord, that I have a few

things *worth* giving. Even if it's a lap to be sat on . . . or the comfort of a warm embrace.

The fire died into glowing embers. It was late as I crawled into bed. I had wept, but now I was smiling as I said, "Good night, Lord." I was a thankful man.

Thankful I had taken time to reflect.

Deepening Your Roots
Jeremiah 17:7 and 8; Psalm 63:5–6; Philippians 2:1–11

Branching Out
1. Take a drive into the country and buy a bag or a crate of apples. Give them all away to those you see in the next forty-eight hours.
2. Give sacrificially today to someone else, but don't tell anyone what you did.
3. Find a beautiful tree and sit under it for awhile. Spend some time thanking God for the people He has brought into your life. List some of their names.

Growing Strong
How's your world? Feeling insignificant? Lost among the masses? Forgotten? I feel that way, too, somedays. It happens every time I look at life from my vantage point rather than God's. How's your perspective today? Are you leaning on God and asking Him to give you His outlook?

Conclusion

Some verses from the Bible make us smile. We have enjoyed them together as we considered a few such verses through the pages of this book. Some references are penetrating and convicting as they cause us to look into the mirror of truth and face facts. We've considered a number of those, too. Others are comforting, giving us hope to go on, regardless. A few introduce us to brand new scenes we'd never seen before. Maybe that has happened as you've worked your way through these pages.

There is one verse, however, that never fails to take us by the shoulders and shake us awake. It comes to my mind because it draws upon a word picture of seasons to make its point. You may recall reading it before.

"Harvest is past, summer is ended,
And we are not saved" (Jeremiah 8:20).

Does that describe *you?* If so, may I suggest that you come to terms with this need. Seasons follow a cycle: winter, spring, summer, autumn . . . so that the earth might enjoy all the things its Creator designed for it to enjoy.

Your life is, in many ways, the same. Multiple seasons, not a long, monotonous marathon of pointless futility; but variety, peaks and valleys, change and color. How tragic to move through the seasons without realizing their ultimate purpose! And what is that?

Go back to the verse. Read it aloud. The purpose is obvious: that we might *be saved* . . . that we might not trust in ourselves but in Jesus Christ, our Creator Lord . . . and, in doing so, receive from Him the assurance of abundant life now and eternal life forever.

Throughout this book I've been truthful with you. Now it's your turn to be truthful with yourself. Are you absolutely certain that you possess His gifts of forgiveness and purpose? You can have that assurance if your traveling Companion through the year is the Son of God. He alone can give meaning to the cycle as He enables you to grow strong in all the seasons of your life.

FOOTNOTES

1. Charles L. Allen, *You Are Never Alone* (Old Tappan, New Jersey: Fleming H. Revell Company 1978), pp. 145–146.
2. Cathy Trost and Ellen Grzech, "What Happened When 5 Families Stopped Watching TV," *Good Housekeeping Magazine*. August 1979, pp. 94, 97–99.
3. Urie Bronfenbrenn, "TV and Your Child," *Christian Medical Society Journal*, Haddon Robinson, ed. (Richardson, Texas: Christian Medical Society, 1978), p. 7.
4. Bronfenbrenn, p. back cover.
5. Philip G. Zimbardo, "The Age of Indifference," *Psychology Today*, August 1980, p. 72.
6. Zimbardo, p. 74.
7. John Bartlett, ed., *Familiar Quotations* (Boston: Little, Brown and Company, 1955), p. 475.
8. Shel Silverstein, *The Giving Tree* (New York: Harper and Row, 1964).